T3-BEA-529

Space–Time–God

Space
– Time
– God

by RONALD W. McNEUR

THE WESTMINSTER PRESS
Philadelphia

LIBRARY OF CONGRESS CATALOG CARD NO. 61-9988

PRINTED IN THE UNITED STATES OF AMERICA

To
LYNDA

Contents

Introduction

On Wanting to Be God

"Man is the being whose project is to be God," [1] wrote Jean-Paul Sartre and not only demonstrated the relevance of the Fall to the whole existentialist anthropology but also in a sentence expressed the basis of the problem of the latter part of the twentieth century. We live in an age when man's neurotic anxiety to be God is given more scope than perhaps in any other age of history. Patterns and attitudes of pseudo divinity that developed in the virile adolescence of our scientific era are still formative symbols for our age, although the rash confidence of adolescence has now been replaced by the uncertainty of experience and maturity. The early-morning dream of scientific utopia has been driven away by the blaze of atomic light, but Bertrand Russell can still write of the task of scientific man: "Let us get on with the job of fertilizing the desert, melting the Arctic ice, and killing each other with perpetually improving technique. Some of our activities will do good, some harm, but all alike will show our power. And so, in this godless universe, we shall become gods." [2]

When man striving to be god ends in despair with Sartre or adopts a vague nostalgic longing with Russell; when man, having destroyed the Transcendent, as Jaspers clearly recognizes, goes forward with arrogance and pride, or, in true Camus style, without hope, there is need for some theological discussion. When Professor Dorn sketched a twenty-four-hour graph that reduced the significant life of man to three tenths of a second before midnight and the giant telescopes probe out into thousands of light years of space, it is time for religious re-evaluation.

In our twentieth century the theological voices have been heard. Barth has thundered forth the dogma of the Christian faith with zeal; Brunner, Niebuhr, and others have sought to relate the faith of man's life to the field of ethics; Bultmann has entered into the discussion of the significance of twentieth-century thought in the exegesis of Scripture; and Tillich has become the apologist for the faith at the court of modern scientific man.

The significance of an apologetic for the Christian faith has become distorted by our use of the word "apology," which in popular language assures a rather craven confession of guilt and a plea for forgiveness for which extenuating circumstances are usually claimed. We should remind ourselves that the apology is an affirmative "case on behalf of." It is not a servile appeal to sackcloth and ashes. It is the honest plea of the defendant, who, although he may be under arrest, must be assumed innocent until the moment he is judged. The apologist steps forward boldly in the time of challenge and accusation.

This book stands as an apologist for the Christian faith. It is not willing to accept the traditional inherited twentieth-century concept of religion, but it claims that the true heritage of the Christian faith has a relevance that has been overlooked in the confident cultural optimism of religious twentieth-century man. It is also unwilling to allow to modern scientific man the extravagant claims that have been made on his behalf.

It will seek to reassert, then, even in the modern loss of the transcendent, that God is God. It will claim that man, despite his satellites and jet bombers, is definitely man. Twentieth-century Adam is still Adam in spite of his arrogance and pride. Perhaps it is by these very assertions that he affirms his birthright. Here, God is God, not the Transcendent Person of the deists or theists, but God is God in the context of the cosmos, the ongoing power of creativity, and the divine quality of concern. He is the God revealed in Jesus who is the Christ. In this book man is man, striving like Adam to have wisdom, to know good and evil, and to be like God.

Apart from the recognition that scientific hypotheses have changed the culture in which we live, no apology is made for scientific man who is more and more becoming a mechanic of the structure that he has defined. The apologia is made that among all the " ologies " of scientific man recognition be given to him who is the " Logos," Jesus the Christ.

I would express appreciation to the mathematicians who led me from pure mathematics to physics, and to the physicists who led me out of physics toward theology, and to my family, parishioners, friends, and professional theologians who have guided me from an abstract to an " existential " theology.

1

Fact and Faith

Objectification

The process of objectification is deadening in any field. Study the blueprints of a modern jet plane or read the mathematical equations of its power and thrust, and unless you have the power of imagination and experience to transfer these to an actual living situation, you will not even have a picture of the gleaming arrow that thrusts its way across the sky and breaks the stillness with its thunder roll of fractured sound. Read through a counselor's analysis of a family situation, and although you may sense the difficulties that he has found, you will not be able to recapture the subtle anxieties and personality tensions that have developed across the years, and you will certainly be an infinite distance from the pulse of life that has created, molded, and disrupted the personal relations. The counselor can point to the failure to maintain a family budget that has contributed to the loss of confidence. He can call attention to inadequacies of personality, to unsolved conflicts of background, to lack of consideration and ignorance of the continual need for adjustment. But he can never analyze or capture in his report the slow atrophy of hope, the gradual disintegration of courage, or the blurring of vision. His analytical scalpel can never probe deep enough to lay bare the cancer of selfishness whose ponderous growth has eventually crushed the life out of love and left nothing but the broken framework.

To analyze and objectify is the very process of thought, but while we do, this life with its vitality and mystery steals quietly away, unnoticed and forgotten. The living situation, carrying with it the warmth of promise or the coldness of decay, refuses to be made the object of our examination. It will not stoop low enough to permit itself to be made the prisoner of our mind. The intimate pattern of personality development, the delicate fabric of appreciation from the unexpected encounter to the creative response, the gentle whisper of eternity within the soul of every man, the instantaneous response to beauty, the calm endurance that we call patience, the unpredictable power called courage that can transform chaos into ordered achievement, cannot be objectified. And with all these, the mysterious process of believing takes its primary place. Delicate, sensitive, existential, it is more intimately related to the very spark of life than any other human quality. Belief as the power of the pulse beat of life can never be removed even by the most careful surgery. All that is found is the structure, the empty shell from which the owner has departed.

The systematic application of the objective method has cleared away all the traditional gods from man's pantheon. For centuries man recognized elements of deity in all aspects of life and in the childhood days of the race peopled his world with gods. But it is no longer possible for man to worship the god of the air, for example, when the atmosphere has been effectively analyzed and its movements charted. The gods of sun and moon have abdicated before the cold objectivity of man's astronomy, and even the demons of sickness have been forced to flee before his developing medical knowledge. It is not surprising that even the deity of man's mature monotheism was finally found to be superfluous. Slowly God was forced back from involvement in man's affairs until he took his refuge in space. The giant telescopes search for him without success, and he is declared to be nonexistent, which in the language of the objective observer means unreal.

This vacating of the pantheon and even of heaven itself is an automatic and natural result of the continuous application of the objective method and the assumption that this method is the sole criterion of reality. In any truly religious statement God is recognized as being nongraspable, nonanalyzable, nonobjectifiable. It is impossible for man to hold him at arm's length and describe his structure in syllogism or equation. The original assumption that God could be objectified immediately classifies the search as futile.

Science is the method and attitude of mind by which we handle and manipulate things. Things are entities that we can objectify, analyze, and grasp with our hand or mind. But if we do not make the assumption that objectifiable things are the only reality, then we must allow for other qualities of being which cannot be the subject of our scientific study and yet are real. Indeed, if we allow that the objective thing is just the one facet of reality that we can observe, then the door is opened to a much richer involvement in life than in the antiseptic barrenness of the scientific laboratory. For to take this step is to change the image of man in relation to reality from that of the detached spectator to that of the involved person. It is true that he has always been both, but the emphasis has been so strongly placed upon his role as detached observer that little allowance has been made for the fact that by his presence as observer he is involved. His energy, mental powers, time, and money have been so completely dedicated to his detached scientific study that his participation has scarcely received any recognition.

Man is a creature who is born to believe. He cannot escape his involvement, and this involvement is set in patterns of belief. Man continually believes, as continually and automatically as he breathes. By the unconscious process of breathing he maintains his continuity in history, and by the unconscious process of believing he sets himself in a meaningful place in that continuity.

Belief in this sense does not mean the acceptance of propositions that begin, " I believe that . . ." ; for the basic assumption of such a statement is that what is believed can eventually be proved by the tools of the objective method. It is a statement of assumed fact that either has been proved and is accepted on authority or is capable of proof if necessary. In either case, " I believe that . . ." is a statement of conditional acceptance of a fact or a group of facts that are provable if the necessary data is available. It is possible for a person to say, " I believe that the world is round " or " I believe that an object falling under the force of gravity will accelerate at thirty-two feet per second per second " without having collected the data, but he knows that, as he accepts the authority of others in this matter, he could conduct his own proof if he so desired.

Belief, as it is used in this discussion of man and his gods, is of a different dimension. It is expressed in the creeds of the church as " I believe in . . . ," and it expresses worship, involvement, commitment, and dedication.

Man is a believing creature. The modern pantheon may not contain the gods of old, but it is filled with other deities in whom modern man believes. Even if he declares that he does not believe in God, he is surrounded by the idols of his own creation, or by the half-gods standing in the half-light, to which he has committed his life, to which he dedicates his creative power, and which he worships. In this modern pantheon resides the god of the objective method, the god of the mechanical process, the god of national power, the god of progress, the god of social status, and the god of power. To these and other lesser deities modern man has dedicated his very being. There is no need for him to set a special time or place for them to be worshiped, nor does he need a special order or service. Man's worship of his deities is implicit in his every action, and his commitment is expressed in every waking moment.

Man's lack of interest in the religious side of his nature has meant that he was willing to commit himself unconsciously to whatever god best suited the development of his objective process. The twentieth century has become the playground of ideologies and cults to which man as an individual or in the mass has been willing to dedicate his life. Some of these have been benevolent, whereas others have been demonic, turning the advance of man's knowledge in upon himself with violent hatred.

The Adoration of the Fact

It is important to recognize that the concepts that we hold in our minds concerning the nature of God are thought symbols compiled from many sources and that almost all of them are interpreted to us through the experiences of our fathers and the traditions of our culture. There is always the danger that we harden these thought symbols into stereotypes and clothe them with the halo of sanctity. A tragic step is taken when these sanctified and stereotyped symbols of God are regarded as God. The man who does this has blasphemously imprisoned God in his own limited thought symbols and has refused to allow himself to remain open to new understanding from the divine.

During the period of scientific rationalism, which has been the hallmark of our recent culture, the temptation to neglect the nature of symbols has been especially strong. We have made fact the sole criterion of truth. Popular theological thought has been especially bedeviled by the demand that theological truth be presented as fact if it is to receive any consideration from the educated twentieth-century man. The result has been that the symbols of religious thought have been interpreted in a literal way and God has been presented in stereotyped thought patterns stripped of their symbolic power by the objective factual method of interpretation.

The argument follows this pattern. Since the Bible is the Word of God, it must be true. If what is written in the Bible is true, it must be fact. Then the world created in six days is a fact and thus is true. Man created in the image of God is a fact and as a fact is reversible. God is then like man only in a super way. His dwelling place is in heaven. The symbolic vision of John in The Revelation is conveniently factualized to give a clear description of this objective city in the sky. Related to this is the happy and factual description of God as " the Ancient of Days," which completed a popular concept of the Christian idea of God for scientifically oriented man. God was a venerable old man sitting upon a throne up in heaven. This turned out to be a very convenient thought-symbol-fact for modern man because it fitted perfectly with the power structure system of his society. God became cast in the category of a superior-type president of the board of directors and Jesus sat at his right hand as a special advocate for man. It was then thought to be religious to state, " I believe in *a* Supreme Being " or " I believe *that* there is a God."

When this step was taken the whole context of religious discussion was set in a scientific objective frame of reference. Deism and theism became patterns in which man considered himself to be religious. Agnosticism and atheism were considered to be irreligious. The religious man declared that there is a God, a Supreme Being, and set out to prove this by every means of the objective-rational method, and the irreligious man stated that there was no such thing as a Supreme Being and sought to establish the proof of his claim. The quest of the Supreme Being was found to be extremely difficult as also was the proof of his nonexistence because no one knew the necessary tools by which to establish and examine his presence.

The result was an uneasy compromise in which moralism and ethics became the basic concern of religion. The religious man was apparently willing to demote Jesus to the position of the perfect man, curiously overlooking the fact that he was crucified by a combination of the civic and religious leaders of his day, and to accept the Bible as the authoritative text for moral guidance, bypassing the fact that it includes records of the most immoral acts. The irreligious man, oscillating between a blatant atheism and a nostalgic agnosticism, was willing to table the whole question of the Supreme Being and to accept certain elements of religious moralism because of their obvious relevance to the structures of his society.

The battle between science and religion was fought largely in these categories. Religious people, fearful of losing their faith, defended their concepts as facts and insisted in interpreting the Bible literally as factual truth. Then, to compensate for a vague uneasiness as to the adequacy of this interpretation, they developed a strong emotional content in their commitment to these facts of faith. The scientist opposed and denied these facts. He could find no valid proof, and his continued investigations yielded him no suggestion of their factual authenticity. So obsessed was he with his own search for factual truth that he had no time to recognize the valid place of symbolic thought. But even so, his negative statement was sound. The theological statements of the Bible are not observable, scientifically analyzable facts. They are symbols pointing to a mystery that our minds can never grasp, hold, and manipulate.

We now recognize that the question about the existence of a Supreme Being was shelved, not because of man's inadequate knowledge, but because it was an inadequate question. It was a question framed entirely within the categories of the objective method, and the answers given were also set in that context. Now we realize that both question and answers were meaningless, for God is of such a nature that he cannot be included within this method of examination. We are also aware that man will worship. And when the God revealed in Jesus Christ was effectively abstracted from his vital contact with life, man turned to other gods, to which he dedicated himself. Specifically the manlike image of the Ancient of Days sitting upon a throne in his golden heaven must now be frankly recognized by religious people as being not a fact but one of the symbol images that men have used when they have tried to express their thoughts about God. Although this thought symbol is still prevalent in our minds, both for the devout who pray to him and for the atheist who denies him, it is an unsatisfactory thought symbol for our age. Our century is busy recasting its own concepts of time and space, and a thought symbol of God that insists on using categories of time and space that we have found to be inadequate is by the nature of the case an inadequate symbol.

Atheism as Revolt

Our era of scientific advance produced many atheists. This is understandable. The concept of God that they inherited included within it an understanding of nature, matter, man, and the universe that they sincerely and successfully challenged. Believers, faced with the apparent destruction of God, defined him in direct opposition to the claims of the new knowledge. He was the God who created the world in six days; who made the first man, Adam; whose throne was the heavens; who kept the record in the book of life; and who would bring time to an end and summon mankind before his throne for the Final Judgment presumably in the calculable future. Although the whole of the new scientific advance was challenged, the theory of evolution both of the world and man became the point where the issue was most sharply defined. The battle was fought under an ambiguous flag.

In their antagonism religious people brought peripheral aspects of the general Christian doctrine and made them central, while the scientists, no longer able to accept these symbols, and therefore automatically defined as atheists, produced a banner with the same symbols interpreted in forms and colors of the materialist philosophy. Swinburne composed the hymn of praise of " Glory to Man in the Highest, for Man Is the Master of Things," and the blueprint of utopia was prepared to be actualized in the near future. Man in his evolutionary ascent would come by nature and reason to glorious heights of achievement. Science alone was able to deal with man's problems. It is true that it was recognized that by the nature of things man and his world were doomed to extinction in the immense death of the solar system, so that everything would eventually be destroyed; but Bertrand Russell summed up the stoic courage of the evolving godless man by declaring that only on the firm foundation of unyielding despair can the soul's habitation henceforth be safely built.

Man is continually endeavoring to define God in categories of his own understanding. In one sense this is all he can do if he is to speak of God at all. The danger and the temptation is that he regards his definition of God as God. The man who inherits a concept of God as the divine orderer but in the course of his life is involved in personal or national disorder is faced with three possibilities. Either he dispenses with the idea of God; or he continues on in half belief, acknowledging that God is order, but the life he gives is disorder; or he recognizes the inadequacy of his idea of God and with open mind lets his concept of God grow in the experiences of his life. This parallels the experience of most people in the whole realm of ideas. They receive certain concepts from their parents, teachers, and society. As they grow, the experiences of challenge, opportunity, suffering, success, and failure force them to reject, re-evaluate, and adjust these concepts so that they can live their own life in their own time. No area of knowledge can resist these changes; indeed, we have now come to expect them especially in all fields of technological knowledge and, indeed, in philosophy.

In religion there is a strange misconception that takes the following line of thought: because God is defined as not subject to change, therefore, our ideas about God must not change either. This is not only a misconception, it is direct blasphemy; for it equates our ideas about God with God himself. We must always realize that our thoughts about God are merely the expression of an awareness of that reflection of his being which we find both hidden and revealed in the world he has created and in the record by sensitive and inspired men from whom has come the record of Scripture. And even this sacred record, we are aware, has to be understood in the context of its time and continually reinterpreted into the context of the present.

It is common experience that the child who grows up in a very restrictive religious environment, who may be loud in his praises and frequent in his amens at the age of twelve, may very easily be an avowed atheist by the age of twenty. Indeed, in a way, this is a much healthier attitude than that of the person who, faced with the problem of correlating his traditional limited concept of God with the development of human knowledge, escapes into religious schizophrenia and with one part of his being thrills at the exploits of our technological age and with the other worships the God who has not yet matured to the scientific age or even to a Copernican cosmology. But the atheist should not allow his emotional involvement to cloud the fact that the God whom he denies is only a human interpretation of the eternal God. The God whom he denies is not God in his reality, but the idea of God that was presented to him in shackles of sanctified thought from the minds and religious experiences of his fathers. The sincere cry of the atheist rightly understood is often a cry demanding God's freedom from the blasphemous bondage of man's definitions set forth in the cultural patterns of his age.

Toward a New Symbol

All men are in some sense religious; all men have an awareness of the whisper of eternity within their being; all men, as Calvin said, have some knowledge of God. It is often vague, fragmentary, encrusted with religious clichés or imagery without much meaning, but the awareness is there. In our time we can classify three large groupings. Together stand the avowed atheists and the extreme religious conservatives. The one denies that there is a God and turns his energy to the exploitation of the material things of this world including man, while the other asserts firmly that there is a God and spells out his nature in concepts that are almost meaningless. They are strange companions, but they are united in this: they have both given up the quest and both indirectly and unconsciously witness to the fact that God is. The second large grouping is the religiously indifferent one that exists in the Western world both inside and outside the churches. Look beneath the surface and you will find an uneasy agnostic who is aware that God is in some way much greater than he has ever been able to imagine but in the course of the struggle has given up thinking and drifts with whatever religious or nonreligious tide in which he happens to find himself. The third category, and it is the most significant group, are the searchers. They are sensitively aware of the need to re-express the traditional concepts in new terms and are expectantly alert to God's self-disclosure in the events of history. In our Christian civilization the searcher is to be found, often in disguise, in almost all walks of life. He may be in the robes of ecclesiastical office or an active member of a church; he is in business, professions, in labor; he may be behind prison bars wearing the insignia of the rebel. He may be outspoken or reticent. Frequently he is misunderstood, for he is not fully aware of Him whom he seeks, and may express his ideas in garbled form. But he is aware of the need of change in man's understanding of God.

The rapid developments in man's technological ability and knowledge, and his advances into both the minute and the vast, force us to be involved in a social and cultural revolution. The theological categories of the past century are no longer satisfactory for expressing the relationship that man is involved in in his religious experience. The $E = mc^2$ of Einstein not only split the atom and produced a mushroom cloud over Hiroshima; it also gave the final blow to theological concepts that had slowly been losing their power since the middle of the nineteenth century. In our world there is no longer room for the little God whose only concern is the individual soul's salvation.

In the relation of religion and science we are now in a new era. Religious men have accepted the advances and acknowledged the theories of science as having value. Specifically, a healthy position has been reached in which the real purpose of religious stories has been recognized as being symbolic, so that religion is not bound to defend the scientific concepts of primitive theory. Furthermore, since the battle has ceased, the religious man has once more begun to recognize the central realities of his faith. Scientists have also become aware of the limitations of their field of endeavor. They are dealing with the material and they acknowledge that reality is much more than material. Sullivan can now write as a scientist that "in his work, scientific man is not completely a man." [3] Eddington, Jeans, and Einstein openly acknowledge the mystery with which all our knowledge is surrounded and can recognize the reality of God. Even though their thought forms and speech may be strange to religious ears with terms such as reality being " mind stuff" and the whole of reality being a thought in the mathematical mind of God, this is a great change from the earlier scientific position.

One reason for this change is, of course, the fact that science did not produce the expected utopia. Great though the advances were, they were scientific and therefore superficial. The discovery of the vastness of man's universe has not added significantly to man's understanding of himself or his place in the universe. The interesting discoveries in the nature of matter in its infinitestimal aspect have only given to man another tool that he may now use for tremendous destruction or thrilling creativity.

We live in the age of schizophrenic man. On the one hand, he glories in his hard-won but fantastically rapid control of the materials of his world and bows in reverence before the cyclotron, the jet engine, and the satellite; and on the other, he appeals to God for help from the threats of destruction that come from the adoration of his own creations. But the God to whom he turns has been so firmly set by man in concepts of petty moralism and pious platitudes that He has no relevance for man on the threshold of space. Must we leave man in this divided state with a foot in two separate worlds or can the bold adventurer also be religious? To put it more directly, must the bold adventurer be religiously grounded if his strenuous endeavor is to have meaning and his life to have purpose?

By his vigorous investigation into the nature of his universe man has placed himself in a strange ambiguity. He is the observer whose proud brain can analyze the structures of his world and endeavor to map out the plans that will bring it under his control. With the tool of the objective process in his hand, he manipulates the stuff of his world until he understands its powers and forces it to obey his will. But the very process by which he has sought to rule his world has forced him to abdicate his throne.

The objective method has proved to be both a blessing and a curse. By it man has asserted his power and authority over the materials of his world. The mountains have given up their iron and gold and uranium, the power of water has been harnessed, the oceans have been imprisoned within the lines of latitude and longitude, and even the wonder of the air has been captured by the isobars of the meteorologist. With each successive conquest man has prospered until he is the undisputed ruler of his world.

But this same tool by which he has conquered is also the weapon that threatens his very life. For man himself is a part of the world that he seeks to dominate. The objective process by which he elevates himself to be the lord of the whole earth informs him that he is merely "a temporary chemical episode in the life of one of the minor planets." Man at the moment of his greatest success becomes his own most serious problem. With the blessing comes the curse. Man has manipulated the reality of his world into categories of thingness in order that he may force it to serve his imaginative desires, but he also discovers that he himself is a thing, and the king on the throne of the universe finds himself categorized as just another statistic. Against this he violently rebels, and his rebellion calls into question the validity of the whole objective process by which he has enthroned himself.

Man will not accept the conclusions of the objective process when they concern himself. He will not accept the implications of his space quest that he is an infinitesimal creature adrift in an ocean of space occupying an infinitesimal period in an infinity of time, nor can he agree with the conclusions of his own analytical probing that he is merely a temporary chemical episode.

The history of the twentieth century can be written as the story of man's reaction against his own implied rejection of himself. He is convinced that he has a relevance, significance, and meaning which is not recognized in his own objective analysis. The cultural upheavals of this century are the results of his fumbling attempt to give recognition to this conviction. If he cannot gain recognition for himself, at least he can prove that his community is significant, so he bands together in the most manageable modern unit, the nation, and goes out to prove himself, equipped with the arsenal that he has created by his scientific method. The experiment has proved so disastrous that he now wonders if the next such valiant endeavor to prove himself may not be his last. In a less violent and more subtle attempt to emphasize his worth he also proceeds to overpopulate the world. But even this attempt to assert his creativity in its most intimate form does not win him recognition except in so far as each new person becomes a terrifying statistic in the greatest population explosion of the centuries.

It is very clear that man is not going to prove his significance and meaning by a more intense or more sophisticated application of the objective method. He would merely spotlight more clearly the tragic ambiguity of his position. The solution to his dilemma can come only from the open recognition that reality is not captured by the analytical process of the objective method. The elements of reality that have been differentiated out in the process of his analysis must now be allowed to take their true place.

2

God and Space

God Is Cosmic

One of the most important steps to be taken in presenting the Christian concept of God in our modern world is to re-emphasize the cosmic aspect of his nature. When the writer of Genesis put down the ancient religious folk tale that we know as the Biblical account of Creation, he was making a most significant religious statement. When he stated that out of the void God created the heavens and the earth, he was expressing a religious awareness that still stands even though his scientific picture of the universe has long ago been discarded.

He may or may not have taken literally Jacob's dream of the ladder reaching up to heaven, but certainly he thought of the sky as being close, if not actually within the distance of the ladder. He had no conception of distance. He had never placed strato-cumulus clouds at 3,000 feet or cirrus at 30,000 feet. The distances of the tropopause and the ionosphere from the earth and Saturn a billion miles away had never occurred to him. Yet his religious statement stands. God is the creator of it all, and God saw that it was good. This statement we still make our own, even though we accept the geologist's theory of the development of our world and Eddington's picture of our rapidly expanding universe and the evolutionist's hypothesis of the development of species. The religious statement still stands: God is creator, and he called it good.

The writings of Scripture present God without limits. He forms the earth and the cosmos. By his word are the heavens created and by his power the sun, moon, and stars are given space. The movement of the world, the diurnal variation of dark and light, and time as man knows it, are all within his creative control. Rivers, plants, forests, the minute and the great, animals and man, are all called to stand forth in existence by his word. Solomon, with an interesting use of the symbol of multiuniverses, speaks of God as one whom the heaven or heavens cannot contain, and indicates that God cannot be contained within the limits of man's three-dimensional space. The writer of Ps. 139 witnesses to God's complete freedom from three-dimensional limitations when he writes:

> Whither shall I go from thy Spirit?
> Or whither shall I flee from thy presence?
> If I ascend to heaven, thou art there!
> If I make my bed in Sheol, thou art there!
> If I take the wings of the morning
> and dwell in the uttermost parts of the sea,
> even there thy hand shall lead me,
> and thy right hand shall hold me.
> If I say, "Let only darkness cover me,
> and the light about me be night,"
> even the darkness is not dark to thee,
> the night is bright as the day;
> for darkness is as light with thee.
> (Ps. 139:7-12.)

In poetic symbol also, the psalmist indicates God's freedom from man's final limitation in time, "A thousand years in thy sight are but as yesterday when it is past" (Ps. 90:4).

The God of the Judaeo-Christian tradition is cosmic. All the elements of creation are called into being by his creative and sustaining power. John makes this abundantly clear when he says, " God so loved the *kosmos* that he gave his only Son " (John 3:16).

The concept receives a fuller emphasis in the writings of Paul, who was striving, along with all the early theologians, to find words and concepts to express the amazing wonder of Christ's person and work. Christ is seen not only as the man of Nazareth but the eternal outgoing power of the eternal God. " All things were created through him." (Col. 1:16.)

In Romans, Paul views the whole sweep of the created world and claims that creation itself is spiritually involved, awaiting its fulfillment. All of creation is within the dominion of the God who has revealed himself in Christ, so that nothing in all creation can ever have power to separate us from his love.

These deep religious insights hold true no matter what physical structure we apply to the universe. The flatland of the Hebrews set in water and capped by the domed arch of heaven, the Ptolemaic earth-centered universe, the Copernican sun-centered cosmos, the spherical space of Riemann and Einstein, the expanding universe of Eddington, all these stand within the context of this religious statement.

God as Person

Popular religious thought has tended to neglect the Biblical doctrine of the cosmic nature of God by directing attention to other theological thought symbols. At times these symbols are treated so literally that the cosmic aspect of God's being becomes embarrassing and even unacceptable. One of these central concepts of the Christian faith is that of God as person.

Biblical theology stands firmly against any blind impersonal, mechanical deity. The Christian God is not Brahman; he is not the Prime Mover; he is not an unconscious power or force. He is continually regarded as person. Intelligence, will, and emotion are automatically regarded as being his attributes in Biblical thought. He thinks, judges, plans, acts, and expresses his concern for the Children of Israel and for his creation. The fullest revelation of his nature and purpose is given in the person and work of Jesus Christ. The whole of Christian thought is committed to the belief in God as person.

The temptation and tendency in popular thought is to move from the theological symbol of God as person to the literal statement that he is a person. When this step is taken, the value and meaning of the symbol is lost and God becomes a person, made in the image of man circumscribed by the limitations of finitude. This tendency must be consciously opposed. God can never be defined from the side of man, and the use of analogies drawn from the human situation must always be kept in the category of symbols. Thus when we speak of God as person, when we address him as " thou " or describe him as " he," we must always be careful to include the reservation that we are not speaking of a person in the human sense of the term. The human personality is limited in knowledge, in understanding, in time, in space, in power. The human personality is always limited, often neurotic, usually schizophrenic. None of these limitations apply to the divine Person. Alan Richardson writes:

> We shall find that personality seems to involve limitation only because we think of human personality and assume

> that personality in God must be exactly like personality in ourselves, including its limitations. Such assumptions are quite gratuitous and, as a matter of fact, are not made by Christian thinkers. When the Christian philosopher says that God is personal, he means, of course, that God is not lower in the order of being than we are. Now personality is the highest category that we know; it is higher than organism or mechanism or anything else. When we say that God is personal, we mean that he is *at least* personal: He is doubtless suprapersonal, but, since personality is the highest category that we know, we cannot say what this involves. Indeed, we know so little about personality in men that we shall not, if we are wise, be too confident of our ability to pronounce upon what it must or must not involve for the divine Being.[4]

The area where we most easily apply limitations to God as person is in the categories where we are absolutely limited as persons. The most fundamental of these are space and time. When we pray that he will guide us we automatically imagine that at a certain time and place his guiding hand will lead us and that this time and place will be defined for him as it is for us. It is very easy to assume that, because we were at a certain time and place when we were aware of his mysterious guidance, God was there in the same way as ourselves; that is, that he came to that moment from a preceding moment and to that place from another place. We should be aware that this is a complete misuse of the symbol of God as person. Because we move from one moment to the next in linear time and from one place to another in three-dimensional space does not mean in any way that God is so limited. Biblically speaking, the space-time continuum is itself a creature of his creative power.

Continually this great Judaeo-Christian concept of God as person has been degraded by man's inability to free it from bondage to finitude. Man always wants to put God as person in a place. The place of God is heaven.

It is perfectly in order to extend the symbol of God as person to include a place called heaven where this person is. But it is not legitimate to try to describe heaven's location by means of the measurements of celestial geography.

Upward has always been the symbolic direction of heaven and probably will always remain so, but we should remind ourselves that " up " for a person in the United States is in the opposite direction from " up " for a person in India. Furthermore, we are well aware that when we start sending rockets out beyond the planets they are not going to crash into the walls of heaven, even though they continue for thousands of light years. Heaven is a symbol for the place where God as person dwells, but it must never be enclosed in finitude or given dimensions or a place in three-dimensional space. God is not a prisoner in space. He is cosmic.

Time is intimately joined to space for us. We only know space in time and time in space. We always occupy space and we occupy it in time. We continually live in, and use for our every action, the categories of " before " and " after." We are creatures of the past, to be made in the future, poised delicately on that fleeting razoredge of reality which we call the present. Everything we do is instinct with our bondage to time. God as person is not so limited to and bound by time. Time is also a product of his creative word. When we speak symbolically of him as person and say he planned, he lives, he acts, we must not assume that he has a blueprint of his plans that will be actualized in the future or that he lives in the categories of before and after. These are the categories of human creatureliness, and we blaspheme God if we bind him to the limitations of man.

The Symbol of Space Time

Scientific Space Time. Science adopts an objective attitude to time that makes no judgments concerning value. Each moment, each year, each millennium in this objective view of the time process in space is of equal value. It is as important for the geologist to place the date of formation on a rock deposit that he has mined, even though it be one million years ago, as it is to date the appearance of Plato or Moses or Christ or the First World War. The passage of this time is traditionally marked out by the clock with its regular and completely disinterested beat. It is linear time with no rise or fall in importance but with equal stress placed upon every moment of its duration. In front of the clock a murder may be committed, a town may be destroyed, and equally well a child may be born or a great new charter of freedom signed, but the clock goes on with its steady beat marking out the objective duration of scientific time.

Spatially, science is equally objective. The amount of space occupied by an atomic bomb is no different from that occupied by an artist's model or a golden casket, provided they enclose the same volume. The gas pump will deliver gas without distinction to the high-speed fighter, the rescue craft, the family car, or the old ladies' Coleman stove, and merely note a difference in volume pumped.

A man occupies space. It is of the same nature as any other space and is measured scientifically in the same way. Some men occupy more space than others, but it is still space. Man not only occupies space that he self-centeredly calls his own or himself; he is at the same time limited by that space and eventually is removed from it, and his space is made available for something else.

As a biological entity in the total process of existence, man is just one minute element in this measure of duration and of space. He may rise to fame, so that his name is recorded in encyclopedias; but even there, the first thing of importance after his name that defines the space he occupied will be the dates of his life, which define his position in linear time. The fact that the accepted standards of scientific measurement and relation have been radically revised by the theory of relativity does not substantially alter the nature of this whole approach as far as the scientist is concerned. The method of objectification remains the same. However, the theory of relativity does introduce a new uncertainty. If everything is relative, is there any ultimate standard against which anything can be given significant place and meaning? One hundred eighty-six thousand miles per second as the speed of light, or −273°C as absolute zero, or seventy million light years as the diameter of our universe as determined by the coefficient of the curvature of light may appear to be ultimate; but we are well aware that, although we may use them freely and authoritatively now, another generation may arise that sees its ultimate in quite different measurements.

The scientific approach also assumes a relationship between the events that it observes and measures. This is expressed as scientific causation and appears as the apparently immutable law of cause and effect. Every observable change is the effect from some cause that may be clearly determined if sufficient research is made and the suitable measuring instruments available. In this respect we can speak of the space-time continuum. It is the environment in which changes occur that are bound together by the cement of causality.

Existential Space Time. For living, a different time scale is called into being. This scale depends for its nature upon judgments of value and meaning. In any life there are moments of great importance, usually interspersed with long periods of linear time that have no immediate significance. The dark night of uncertainty, anxiety, and despair that precedes the new day of understanding and joy, the experiences of love, the ecstatic moments of achievement, of new awareness and of unconscious self-giving, all stand out as moments of great worth, and the objective time that separates them vanishes into insignificance.

The same radical revision must also be made with regard to space. Dallas, Texas, Hamburg, Germany, and San Francisco, California, may be widely separated according to our objective view of space; but for the man who was married in Dallas, who almost lost his life in air battles in the sky above Hamburg, and who reached a mature understanding of his life's meaning as he settled in a job in San Francisco, these places are not separated. They are all bound together in his life as a unity in which the scientific view of space has no place.

The new element that is introduced is involvement. This stands in opposition to the objective attitude of science. The customary standards of scientific measurement are thrown aside in favor of relationship. This is a very significant step and one that we should ponder. As long as we take the objective measurements of science as final we in effect define ourselves out of existence. We are merely the observer viewing the occurrences that happen and manipulating them as we are able. But if we are to see these measurements as merely useful tools and existence as a stage in which we are actually involved, life steps out into a new dimension.

Gogarten wrote of history in existential terms when he described history as the presentness of the past in the present. Remembered events, then, are not merely the cold facts that are objectively recorded; they are realities that live now, stepping out of the past and encountering us here and now. The primary space-time words in this thought are " here " and " now." " There " and " then " are used only in a secondary way and only as derivatively related to the here and now. Space time becomes the context of relationship and is the reality.

Theological Space Time. The theological understanding of space time introduces another concept. It assumes that the divine is in some way involved. This can run the whole gamut from the Greek view in which the gods became involved in time and space in a purely arbitrary manner to the Christian view where God is seen as specifically concerned with events in history.

Christian theology takes the space-time continuum seriously. It is real, and the actions and events that occur within it are of real importance. The new and culture-creating thought that came to life in the religion of the early Hebrews was that events in history were actually God at work. The divine was participating. The divine was involved. Far from being a series of meaningless occurrences the events of history were seen as high drama in which God is the chief actor. The significant events are then those in which the leading actor is most clearly seen.

The definitive event that is the basis of meaning and also the key to interpretation is the event of Jesus Christ, his life, his teaching, his death and resurrection. This stands at the "center" of history, giving meaning to its total sweep. Here again a revision is made in our concept of linear time; for this event is declared to be the center, not because it is the linear center, as obviously it comes late in the time scale, but because its power reaches out into the present and lays hold of the soul and being of man. This power is so great that it also draws all elements of history, so that they fall into a meaningful pattern.

Berdyaev presents a theological approach to space time when he writes of history:

> The historical in the real sense of the word brings with it the revelation of essential being, of the inner spiritual nature of the world and the inner spiritual essence of man. . . . The "historical" is by its nature not phenomenal but deeply ontological.[5]

With this thought, new dimensions are called into being. The four scientific dimensions are still used as convenient tools for objective description, but new spiritual dimensions are seen as the true context of reality. Existential terms are called into service. Jesus appeared in the linear scale of time and in three-dimensional space *then* and *there,* but as the Christ he possesses a *hereness* and a *nowness* that is of ultimate significance.

The four scientific dimensions are still relevant, but they do not encompass the total reality. A three-year-old child in drawing a picture of his parents will likely place a large head on two long legs. The reason apparently is that the face is that part of the person which most frequently encounters, praises, or scolds him, and responds to his requests. So the head predominates.

In some such way our four-dimensional space time is related to reality. Theology would recognize that we are limited in our ability to portray the real. The standards that we do use are of some significance, but we must recognize that they are inadequate, distorted, and in no way to be regarded as ultimate. But there are other dimensions that we see included in the concept of divine space time.

Divine Space Time. There are certain theologians who would claim that it is impossible to speak of divine space time. Space and time are the structures of existence and God does not " exist." He, and he alone, is. He is being, he is essence, and to seek to use the concepts of space and time in discussing his nature is to question his infinite and eternal qualities. Thus the early Karl Barth takes the very starting point of his religious awareness as " the infinite qualitative distinction between time and eternity." From the Christian point of view, however, it is important to form some concept of divine space time. Space time is the continuum in which actions occur. It is the area of living. Analogically we must carry it into the divine sphere; for the Christian is convinced that God acts and that he lives. To speak of a God who does not act is to assign God to the far-off Olympian heaven of idealism and to undercut the whole Christian concept of his involvement in history.

Nevertheless, it is also apparent that we must proceed with caution. It is very easy, especially in this technological age, to slip from the concept of divine space time to the assumption that the time we are speaking about is scientific linear time, and that the space is scientific measurable space. Oscar Cullmann in an examination of the Christian concept of time presents this point of view. He makes a strong appeal for interpreting eternity in terms of the " naïve " concept of time.

> Thus time and eternity share this time quality. Primitive Christianity knows nothing of a timeless God. The " eternal " God is he who was in the beginning, is now,

> and will be in all the future, " who is, who was, and who will be " (Rev. 1:4). Accordingly, his eternity can and must be expressed in this " naïve " way, in terms of endless time.[6]

It is this concept of endless time which causes difficulty. It obviously cannot be taken literally to mean the unlimited progression of linear time. Even geometry does not conceive of an endless line, for a line infinitely extended will meet itself at infinity. " Endless time " is of a different quality from infinite linear time.

Cullmann obviously feels a great obligation to take the concepts of time and space as presented in Scripture as definitive. Yet it is also apparent that he finds some of its interpretation embarrassing, especially when he has to bypass the very early Christian tradition that confidently expected the end of time within that generation. Christ would return and those who were alive would be caught up and reunited with God in the air. He also gives no place to the very significant claim of Christ: " Before Abraham was, I am " (John 8:58).

It is generally agreed that there is no obligation laid upon the Christian to accept the scientific concepts of Scripture as definitive. The Bible is a record of God's dealing with man and of man's response. It is not a textbook of science, of sociology, of psychology, or philosophy, although, to those who respond to its story, it gives a definite point of view that directs thought in all these disciplines. But any preacher or Biblical commentator who takes time expounding a text or a chapter of Scripture is interpreting the Biblical terminology into the thought forms of the present in order that the good news of its message may be understood. It is also apparent that the early Christians, who were as limited as we are by time and space, had to use temporal and spatial terminology in giving expression to their life-changing experience. Modern scholars are constantly explaining the situations and environment of Biblical incidents in order to free the basic message from the cultural incidentals of the time, and even conservative scholars take advantage of the Calvinistic principle of divine accommodation to the needs and understanding of the people of the time to make the necessary adjustments in the gospel message to bring out its true meaning. To take the analogies of Scripture and make them definitive and treat them literally is to do an injustice to the thought of the early Christians.

There are a number of developments of thought that can give us some direction in re-evaluating our ideas of divine space time. Paul Tillich has endeavored to bring the understanding of symbol in religious life and language into its perspective. The only statement that he allows as nonsymbolic is that God is being-itself. After this, everything that is said about God is symbolic.

> As we already have seen, God as being-itself is the ground of the ontological structure of being without being subject to this structure himself. He is the structure; that is, he has the power of determining the structure of everything that has being. Therefore, if anything beyond this bare assertion is said about God, it is no longer a direct and proper statement, no longer a concept. It is indirect, and it points to something beyond itself. In a word, it is symbolic.[7]

The whole discussion on the nature of the symbol and symbolic language that follows is an integral part of his thought and is a most stimulating area of study.

Another helpful direction of thought for us who have been trained in objective categories is to become acquainted with the names used for God in the Old Testament. Although the context is always that of God as person, there are names used for God in the Old Testament that immediately turn us away from the temptation to consider him as a person. In the Hebrew he is called El, which means power, or more frequently Elohim, which is the plural form. Both these names definitely discourage us from personalizing God and restricting him to human dimensions. The most holy name is Yahweh, which is never spoken. (Its consonants are in the word " Jehovah " and its vowels are in the word " Adonai " [Lord], which is a dual term.) Yahweh derives from the root of " to be " or " to become."

Hebrew thought is much richer in its concepts of God than the Romans with their *deus,* the Greeks with their *theos,* and the Anglo-Saxons with their simple term " God." At one very significant place in the record of Moses when he asks the name of God, he receives the reply, " I AM WHO I AM," or " I WILL BE WHAT I WILL BE " (Ex. 3:14) . However this is translated, there is involved a very profound awareness of the strangeness, mystery, majesty, and power of God. Here is one who is self-determinative, whose very being defines reality. The fuller examination of the phrase, in so far as this can be done by anyone in our objective structured culture, obviously leads us far away from a person located in one place at one time. Here is " being " in a completely other form than that which we know as human.

That the Jews were aware of this is shown from the reaction expressed in the New Testament narrative when Jesus used this name. In discussing his relation to Abraham, whom the Jews of the first century took as their authority, he stated, " Before Abraham was, I am," and was promptly attacked not for insanity but for blasphemy. There was only one who could utter this statement and utter it in perfect truth. That was Yahweh, the " I AM WHO I AM."

Contrary to popular belief in the evolutionary nature of religious thought, this God of the Old Testament was not always a primitive deity whose nature became known as man progressed culturally. There are insights here far too deep for the understanding of our supposedly mature minds. One aspect that we must immediately reintroduce into our thought is that of the self-determining God who is completely unfettered by our limitations of space and time. In all space he is God and at all times — past, present, and future as we define them — he can say, " I AM."

Another significant approach is made by Prof. Karl Heim, who is concerned with relating the insights of modern science with the thought symbols of theology. In *Christian Faith and Natural Science* he pleads for the rejection of the " two-storied " universe and for the development of new forms of thought to express the truths of the Christian faith. Using the discoveries of modern existential thought, he proposes the possibility of divine space incorporating our measurable space and time. He examines the equations of modern mathematics that use the concepts of multidimensions and of non-Euclidean geometry as it works with curved space that is the basis of our modern cosmology. From this is drawn the recognition that it is perfectly feasible for there to be space in and through the space we occupy that we are unable to recognize, analyze, or even objectify.

For Heim the I-Thou relation that we experience *here* and *now* stands outside all the spatial and temporal dimensions that apply within objective space. The *nonobjective* space of existential relation cannot be analyzed by the objective methods of science. But the structure of this *nonobjective* space gives rise to a conflict between the mutually exclusive claims of I and Thou, each of whom considers himself as the center of space. Here is a basic either/or that is of great concern to Heim. That is the basic problem of what he calls "polar space," and he sees it as applying both to objective and nonobjective space. The only solution to this dialectic position is to assert a unity beyond the polarity of three-dimensional space and unidimensional time. This he achieves by the use of what he calls "suprapolar space." It is described as a "form of being" that is "just as all-present and all-embracing and just as inclusive of the whole of reality as is the case with the polar form of being within which we are confined." [8]

Heim is very careful to underscore two aspects of this thought. The first is in answer to the urgent question that would come from many believers when presented by this new concept. "If the space of God is reduced to a common denominator with the space of this world, is that not a titanic attempt by human thought to make itself master of God and to enmesh him, who is after all 'the wholly other' in the net of our human concepts and categories?"

He strongly claims that this is not so. The being of God remains incomprehensible and shrouded in mystery.

> Just as the language is not the substance of the book itself but the form in which this substance reveals itself to a certain group of readers, so too the suprapolar space, in which God is present for us, is not the reality of God itself. This ultimate quality remains that which is "wholly other," totally incomprehensible and entirely inaccessible to our thought and observation. It confronts us neither as an object, in the way in which solid objects are disclosed to us, or as a Thou, in the sense in which the I and

> Thou confront one another in the polar space. When we speak of the suprapolar space, we cannot be referring to the eternal reality of God itself but only to one aspect, a side which is turned toward us, the only side from which God can be accessible to us, to you and me, if he is willing to disclose himself to us at all.[9]

The second emphasis is that this concept effectively dispenses with the limits of Euclidean space and the Ptolemaic concept of a two-storied world that theology has used mythologically and that, if retained, cannot but produce " double-entry bookkeeping " on the part of scientifically trained man who is not only dishonest but also dangerous. With this concept of suprapolar space the " infinite qualitative distinction " between time and eternity is maintained, but the eternal is no longer set in a distant upper story far off in the cosmos. The approach presented by Heim is thrilling to one who has lived with a foot in both the world of science and that of religion and at times has found the strain almost too much. Heim is dealing with a most important problem of our time, and one that will continue to be discussed, it is hoped, with as much frankness and concern as is shown here.

It is unfortunate, however, that the main concept with which he seeks to break away from the " two-storied " interpretation of reality is itself set in the context of above and below. Although he strives again and again to divest his term " suprapolar space " of three-dimensional space connotations, the term itself automatically suggests this structure. He rejects the attempt to describe eternal reality in similes, borrowed without exception from three-dimensional solid space.

> That is what we are doing when we say, for example, that the eternal reality, which Goethe tells us we must revere, is what is over us; it is " above " the terrestrial world; or, alternately, it lies outside the frontiers of this world;

> whatever emanates from it drops " down from above," like a missile striking the earth's surface and making a hollow space, like a shell hole.[10]

Yet in defining his particular approach he claims that " the whole world form of polarity is transcended " and he gives it the name of suprapolar space. In both these definitive points in his thesis he remains within the phraseology of the two-storied theology, and it is at this point that his thought must be advanced.

The divine space time of which we speak is neither spatial nor temporal in our understanding of these terms. Divine space time stands as a symbol for the reality of God in his cosmic power. It is not primarily a symbol of magnitude but of reality in its essential nature. And reality in its essential nature is God in his being. God is. In and through the whole of the cosmos, God is. He is its ground of being; he is its source of meaning. Divine space time is neither above nor below in the sense of our spatial and temporal terms. It is, rather, in and through and with a dimension of depth, as this carries the sense of penetration.

One of the most interesting attempts to restudy man's relation to reality and to God has been made by Martin Buber. The emphasis is on the primacy of the personal. In his epoch-making book, *I and Thou,* Martin Buber begins:

> To man the world is twofold, in accordance with his twofold attitude.
>
> The attitude of man is twofold, in accordance with the twofold nature of the primary words which he speaks.
>
> The primary words are not isolated words, but combined words.
>
> The one primary word is the combination *I-Thou.*
>
> The other primary word is the combination I-It; wherein, without a change in the primary word, one of the words *He* and *She* can replace *It.*

> Hence the *I* of man is also twofold.
> For the *I* of the primary word *I-Thou* is a different *I* from that of the primary word *I-It*.[11]

Buber's brief book continues with a stimulating description of these two relationships. The one is objective. It is the scientific attitude in which the person is always the observer. The other is the existential relationship of involvement. Although the word " I-It " may be most useful for our control of the material of the universe, the I-Thou relationship is of the very stuff of reality. " All reality is meeting."

Buber, relying greatly upon the traditional mystical aspects of religion, relates the I-Thou experience of reality directly to man's relation with God.

> In every sphere in its own way, through each process of becoming that is present to us, we look out toward the fringe of the eternal *Thou;* in each we are aware of a breath from the eternal *Thou;* in each *Thou* we address the eternal *Thou*.[12]

Although we may not agree with the extreme mysticism that develops in Buber's thought, we must take very seriously his analysis of the two types of attitude and the primacy of the personal. The tendency we have to cast everything in life into the category of I-It is a contributing cause of our present social sickness. When each individual becomes his own center of reality and everything else is objectified, then each man becomes his own god.

The great value of Buber's thought, which has been used and developed extensively by other philosophers and theologians in the last two decades, is that it points us to the place of relationship in our thought of reality. Many implications of the basic Biblical doctrine of God as person can now be seen as we step out of the distortions that result from our endeavor to objectify all things — nature, man, and God — and bring them within our power.

In the continuing discussion of the relation of divine space time to our four-dimensional space time of existence the Christian sees the person of Jesus as the Christ as of central importance. In the historical event of his life is presented to man the relationship of the divine and the human. He is the living actuality of this relationship. Thus the Christian is aware that the significant statements about the relatedness of human space time and its source cannot be stated finally in the terms of mathematical equations or the theories of physics but in the dimensions of personality as they are shown in Jesus as the Christ.

The Christian faith would lead us to a cosmic God who is in and through all things; by whose power all things were created; and by whose providing all things hold their place in existence. Man's mind can never grasp the being of God in his totality. He grows in understanding and in faith as the experiences of life come upon him. He must stretch his thought to grasp the reality that is forced upon him.

Here in our modern age we must expect our minds to be challenged and stretched to grasp the nature of God as cosmic. We are creatures of the atomic age at the time when man's thought is undergoing dramatic changes, and we must allow our personalities to grow religiously as we allow our minds to grow in scientific knowledge. We must catch the concept of the cosmic God or we become poor schizophrenics, advancing to the postgraduate level in our understanding of the external world but leaving ourselves equipped with merely a third-grade religious mentality in our efforts to examine and solve the problems of our own existence.

To believe in the cosmic God is to be aware that the whole of the universe or the universes is under God's creative control. Although we may be profoundly impressed by man's venturing into space, we are aware that from the points of view of the universe, he is like a small child just dabbling his feet in the smallest waves of the vast ocean. And the ocean of space is within God's control. With this thought in mind man will venture forward with confidence and responsibility — with confidence because he realizes that this whole new area of interest is not a disorderly or chaotic realm, although it is completely new to him, and with responsibility because he realizes that he is still within the creative and controlling power of God.

Divine space time is reality in its pure form. The objective space time of science defines the limits in which mankind and his universe are enclosed. The existential frame of reference includes all those occasions in which the divine space time is partially revealed to a person in the things of a four-dimensional context. Theology is man's attempt to interpret these glimpses he has of the real and the enduring and to relate them to the world in which he lives.

I am well acquainted with an artist. I know her physical appearance and I am stimulated and affected by her personality. I also possess a picture that she has painted. The picture is an object on my wall. It has been given reality by her ability to place paint on canvas and express responses and ideas. Every time I admire the painting I am aware of the personality of the painter, not directly or apart from the painting as I was when she first gave it to me, but instinctively and intuitively because qualities of her being are incorporated in her creation.

I use this painting to beautify my office, and its colors blend with the interior decorations. I am inspired by it because it has a mysterious message of its own. It is called " Communion " and is painted in the modern style.[13] Its Kandinski-like swirls and its subtle color relations are the source of continual inspiration. I may misuse the painting. I may place it where its colors clash with its surroundings and destroy its message. I may treat it lightly and employ it as a casual conversation piece. For some people who come into my study the painting has no meaning. It is an object on the wall, but they do not respond to its message and they form no impression or perhaps only a distorted impression of the personality of the artist. But for me the personality of the artist is always there to meet me if I am in the attitude of mind for the meeting. The painting is real. It has a life of its own. But in and through it is the personality of the artist who has given it life.

Illustrations such as these all have their limitations. But they can serve here to throw light on the relationship of space time that we have discussed. The objects, the events, and the experiences that occur and we observe in our four-dimensional space-time continuum are real. They have a life of their own. We can use them or misuse them. They can mean nothing to us or they can be the bearers of an understanding of ourselves and life. They can bring us in touch with the " really real." Situated in our space and our time they can lead us to the awareness of another space-time continuum that cannot be measured by our dimensions and has no relation with them other than that they receive their reality by being in this context.

Barnett points the way at the conclusion of his book, *The Universe and Dr. Einstein.*

> Man's inescapable impasse is that he himself is part of the world he seeks to explore; his body and proud brain are mosaics of the same elemental particles that compose

the dark, drifting clouds of interstellar space; he is, in the final analysis, merely an ephemeral conformation of the primordial space-time field. Standing midway between macrocosm and microcosm he finds barriers on each side and can perhaps but marvel, as St. Paul did nineteen hundred years ago, that " the world was created by the word of God so that what is seen was made out of things which do not appear.[14]

3

Fate or Providence

The Popular Creator

One of the most popular concepts of God's nature is that of creator. Especially is this so of the idea that sees God as original creator and establisher of the laws of nature and morality. Most men will agree to the argument of the First Cause that God set the stage, so to speak, of the universe, called on the actors, and has given them freedom to work out their own parts within the limits that he has originally established within the structures of his creation.

The popularity of this concept in the present day is very understandable when we consider the emphasis that we have given to the scientific and objective study of the so-called laws of nature. We have assumed that nature is mechanical and have had considerable success in cataloging its activities. From an understanding of the infinitesimal in the atom to the infinite in the movement of the stars we feel that we have developed a system that will eventually explain all phenomena and in the end be able to forecast everything, from the process of nature to the movement of the human will.

Another reason for the popularity of this concept is that we think we know what it means to create. We have all made something. Perhaps we are trained in carpentry and have actually built a house or a boat or a cabinet; perhaps we are able to work in metals and have made a machine or a mobile;

perhaps we are interested in buying and selling and in the process we have built a business. Everyone is a creator and has produced something that was not there before. We are very proud of what we create, probably because it is the main thing we do. The artist puts his name on his painting, the builder puts his sign in front of the house he is constructing, the writer signs his book, and parents pass on their names to their children. We all create and we enjoy creating.

It is not surprising that one of the very common questions that we ask is, Who made it? or Who wrote it? or Who painted it? for we know that everything has to be made by somebody. From the reputation of the maker we can often determine the quality of the creation. It is quite normal that one should ask of the world and the universe, Who made it? To this very normal question the understandable reply is, God created the world and the universe. For many people this is, in effect, the definition of God. Just as we do not know Mozart or Van Gogh or Shakespeare, but we know and enjoy their works, so, such people would say, we do not know God, but we can still see and appreciate his works. God is the name that is then given to the mysterious beginning of the whole process that brought the universe, our world, and ourselves into existence.

The assumption basic in this approach is that God is now unnecessary even if he still "exists," just as Mozart, Van Gogh, and Shakespeare are no longer necessary in order for us to understand, appreciate, and use their works. We understand the rules of the art form they used and have a most enjoyable time explaining and demonstrating to one another what they meant to say in their creations. Indeed, we sometimes feel that even if the artists were to return to life, they would not understand their own productions as well as we do.

The Christian does not accept the above assumption, namely, that God is unnecessary even if he still " exists." In fact, the god whose nature would fit into this assumption is in no way the Christian God. Therefore, this popular concept of the Creator God has to be treated with extreme reserve by those who would profess the Christian faith.

We must, first of all, underscore that no type of reasoning enables us to " prove that God exists." We may imagine that we can go back step by step in logical reasoning to show that anything in the world depends upon some former thing or person for its presence until we come to the final step that is at the very beginning of time and say " God created." He is the " First Cause." We may think that we have proved God; but even a child, or especially a child, can see the flaw in our logic. Almost every child has insisted on continuing this process of thought and has embarrassed his parents by asking the perfectly logical question, Who made God? The question shows us that there is really no logical reason for us to stop at the god who created; indeed, he could just as easily have been brought into being for the purpose of creating our universe, our world, ourselves, as not.

Neither this so-called " proof " of the existence of God, nor other " proofs " that point to the order of nature, the universality of belief, the strange concept of right that dwells in the mind of every man, or the fact that everything seems to have a purpose, can ever effectively prove God. There is no way by which we can follow through a line of reasoning in which the concluding line is, " Therefore, God exists," and proudly place a Q.E.D. at the end before we close the book. Whatever we have proved here is certainly not God. The Christian does not believe *that* " God exists." God is not to be included in the groups of existing things. He is the source of all things that come into existence and they have true reality in relation to him. But God in his being is not a thing among other things in existence.

A gigantic red herring has been drawn across the path of Christian theology with the obsession of proving that God exists. From time to time arguments for the existence of God have been the precious treasure of the Christian apologist. Even today Neo-Thomism and extreme fundamentalism become uncomfortable bedmates in this atmosphere of blasphemy. For blasphemy it is. It lowers God down into the category of thingness and crucifies him afresh on the cross of objectivity.

I may believe *that* George Washington was the first president of the United States. I may believe *that* the component parts of water are hydrogen and oxygen. I may believe *that* Jesus was born in the year 4 B.C. or whatever year scholars assign. But all this is a totally different thing from the statement of faith. I believe *in* God, Father, Son, and Holy Spirit. And " I believe *in* " is the only phrase used in the creeds of the church. " I believe *that* " is the language of objectivity and its proposition accepted on the basis of proof or some type of external authority. I believe *in* is the language of context. This is the language of faith and worship and true life.

It is unfortunate that the atheistic writers of the present day confine themselves to this battleground, although the battleground was already defined by the church and the rationalistic philosophies of the past era. And it is unfortunate that now the phalanx of the logical positivist camp has marked out its place in the same field, while the church seeks to strengthen its already weakened forces. The tragedy is that no matter how vehement may be the charge and the countercharge, no matter how sharp may be the rapier thrust of style or cannonade of proof, it is all a game of tin soldiers who may equally well be left on the field overnight or put away in the box until next Christmas and nothing of significance has occurred. The tragedy is that men dedicate their lives to this battle and effectively prove for themselves with Nietzsche that " God is dead " and commit suicide in insanity, or with Camus, declare that life is absurd and shun suicide, for it denies the absurdity, or they prove to themselves that God exists and double their roles as dogmatic theologians with that of positivistic scientists and blast H-bombs to his glory in the most colorful display in human history. The disaster is, and this is where the battle over God's existence becomes tragic, that after the blast comes the fallout, and the fallout can be deadly.

Therefore, we must proceed with caution in the use of analogy in describing God as creator.

When we speak of God as creator and think in terms of our own activity in making things we are using an analogy. We are taking an experience that we know and are transferring this to an area of life that we do not completely understand and are trying to explain. Analogy, metaphor, and simile are very common methods of explanation, but we must realize their limitations. Analogies can be used only by the mature mind that has learned a sense of restraint in the use of imagination and knows where to draw the line. Parents soon realize how careful they must be in the use of analogy in the presence of their children. The man who speaks of his acquaintance as a road hog should not be surprised to find his five-year-old son upon meeting this person, wrinkling his eyes in an attempt to see the snout or the tail, or the trotters hidden in suède shoes. The analogy is the cartoonist's livelihood, and it must be carefully used or it completely distorts reality. The father should now realize that when he used the term " road hog " he should have defined the limits of his thought. He did not mean that this person looked like a road hog. He did not mean to imply a snout or a tail or trotters. All he meant was that as we usually consider hogs to be selfish, greedy, and unmannerly, so this person in his car displayed the same qualities. When one considers any of our other analogies, it is apparent that limits are automatically and unconsciously applied in them all.

We must be equally careful with the human analogies that we apply in our understanding of God or else we delude ourselves with a peculiar cartoon fabrication of our own immaturity. As soon as we call God creator, we must at the same time explain that he is not bound, as a human creator is, by the fetters of time, space, and materials.

In general, the human creator completes his creation and then enjoys the fruits of his labors. At a certain time the house is built, the open house is held, and the family then lives in and enjoys this new creation. There comes a time in the painting of a picture or the writing of a book or the composition of a sonata when the creator stops his work and signs his name. The work is completed. This is true of all our projects. For we are finite. There is an end to us and so we apply an end to our creative plans. But God is infinite. It is wrong to put an end to his creative process. He is not circumscribed by the limits of time.

However, by misuse of this analogy men have forced themselves into cartoonlike misconceptions about God. This is true of both the secularist and the religious person. The secularist, with a strong emphasis upon science, will acknowledge God as creator. In fact, it is necessary for him to believe in God or else his whole scientific order is called into question. In general, it is held that at the beginning God created the universe and the world, just as a builder creates a house, and then set everything in order for the family of man. He then retired to enjoy his creation and let it run according to the laws that he had established.

At one stage it was regarded as a religious victory when a scientific theorist acknowledged that he had thought back as far as he could in the orderly process of evolution and that he had to admit that there must have been some creative action by an almighty creative power to set the initial process into operation. It was hailed as a great religious truth when the biologist, tracing back the development of life to the earliest form, finally came to an impasse with the question of the origin of the first spark of life, and acknowledged, often with hesitancy and embarrassment, that the first spark of life must have been created by God or some supreme being. But even logically and scientifically the step could have been taken long before to the same conclusion, that if the orderly process of scientific thought had any merit or purpose, then there must be an order that is all-inclusive, and therefore, there must be an orderer. Otherwise, everything falls into the spinning wheel of chance — even the amoeba, even the world, even the scientist — and chance is meaningless.

The thought that the Creator God set the process of the universe in motion and then retired to his celestial dwelling has played a special part in the development of religions. When you move into a house you do not want the builder living in with you, continuing to add to the structure while you are there. You want him to be far away and to come back only at your invitation when there is something that needs his particular attention. This is the way we have often thought of God as creator. This is true of many denominations and sects of Christendom that have established the clear-cut rules by which God's Spirit is defined as a type of spiritual experience, and for others it is a particular type of social conformity and outward spiritual attitude that was the rule by which one aligned oneself with the original purpose of the Creator. But the divine Creator himself is removed from the scene. His work is done. All that now remains is to come to an understanding of his purpose and to direct all social planning, scientific development, and spiritual attitudes in keeping with the set laws that he has incorporated in his created universe.

In both these attitudes, the scientific and the religious, there is faulty use of the analogy. If it were children who were making the error, it would be understandable and would even be suitable material for a cartoon. But the error is made by mature men, and the comedy turns out to be a tragedy with self-righteous and self-reliant man deluding himself that this distorted analogy is the truth.

Fate

In his play *Murder in the Cathedral,* T. S. Eliot pictures a group of the ordinary people of Canterbury receiving back their archbishop from exile. They seem to have a premonition of the disaster about to befall him and plead with him to go back to France. They urge him not to involve them in events beyond their understanding and control. They want to live quietly and securely. And as they express their hidden terror of the dangers and disasters that may come, they call themselves the " small folk drawn into the pattern of fate."[15]

Here is an imaginative phrase that we all understand. In any time of disaster we feel like leaves before a March wind being tossed around by forces that we cannot even understand, let alone control. A man loses his job, perhaps because production has been discontinued, or because along the way someone has directed him into work that he did not enjoy and in which he could never succeed. However it occurs, in a situation where security of income is threatened, we feel that we are " small folk drawn into the pattern of fate."

A speeding car cuts down an innocent pedestrian; a flash flood destroys homes and drowns families; a bomb is dropped in a civilian area and kills and maims women and children whose only guilt is that of geographical location; a child born with great rejoicing in 1930 finds as he matures to manhood that he has arrived just in time to be involved and killed in the Korean war; the prospects of a great career and happy family life are destroyed by the ravages of a fatal disease. Let any of these occur and the stunned mind can do little more than turn in despair and whisper " fate."

It has been so down through the centuries of time. The young Roman involved in the capture and fall of Rome, inheritor of an empire in decay, surely wondered why he had been called upon to give his life's energy and ability in participating in the death throes of an empire that had known such heights of grandeur. The mother whose children were all destroyed in the medieval plagues or whose sons were drowned in the tides of conflict must certainly have wondered what freak of fortune decreed that she would exist in such a troubled time and be forced to bear her disaster in loneliness. What sort of pattern of life was formed in the minds of unsuspecting Negroes carried off to slavery and torture? What philosophy would be expressed by modern prisoners of war, forgotten and forsaken in the slave camps of a former enemy?

Are you a fatalist? This is a question that is frequently

asked and surely always has been asked by men and women when the disasters and agonies of existence pressed hard upon their minds.

The door that separates fate from fatalism is a very fragile door and the wall that divides them is thin, but the atmosphere on the one side of the wall is vital and on the other is deadly.

In the Army camp in which I was trained there was a gas chamber. It was a hut, partly underground, set aside from the rest of the camp in a shaded grove of eucalyptus trees. I can remember marching down to the hut with the company for a gas-mask drill. We stood in the speckled shade of the giant trees that all but shut out the brilliant sunshine of the hot summer day. The pungent fragrance of the eucalyptus trees made the air seem fresh and clean. Then we put on our gas masks and walked into the hut. It was a very narrow door and a very thin wall that enclosed the dimly lighted room into which the gas was pumped. But that door separated light from darkness, freshness from decay, and life from death.

Just as thin but just as definitive is the dividing line between faith and fatalism.

Both attitudes seek to deal with the totality of life. And life in its totality is a many-faceted and mysterious thing. There is a strangeness in birth that is neither requested nor desired into an environment that is already formed. From the very beginning there are forces at work upon the personality of a growing child that contain elements of a total world attitude of which as yet he has not the slightest conception. Before he has reached the age of five and has actually formulated the basic questions that his being has been asking since he saw the light of day, there has been presented to him in sugar-coated form, with the authentic stamp of parental approval, embryonic philosophies of life, of the world, of race, of career, and of personal relations. These he must take, for there is nothing else for him to take, to satisfy the yearning of his spirit, and they mold his personality and make him what he will become.

Certainly, he may rebel against this or that element in his maturing years, but he can never turn aside from it all or he would be rejecting his very self. Life automatically sweeps him along through the years of schooling where he is indoctrinated with the current educational philosophies of the country and the culture into which he has been born. He comes to maturity and marries a woman who happened to be in the environment when the deep urges of life gripped him, and they place together their different personalities with their hopes and their despairs and seek to reach a livable compromise that is tangibly represented in their child. His career and his economic position depend largely on what his world and culture places before him in the way of opportunity and incentive. Then finally he comes to the farthest limit of life's stage and takes his departure in loneliness or in acclaim, in pain and agony, or in the quietness of sleep. He dies. He is buried and is seen no more.

It is easy to project a life onto a flat two-dimensional canvas, to examine its beginnings, its peaks of success, and its valleys of failure leading eventually to its end, and to scrawl " Fate " across its chart before throwing it into the garbage can of history. But to say " Fate " is to remove the very dimension that makes life life. To say " Fate " removes the dimensions of height and depth in which are courage and hope, anxiety and despair, even the ability to make decisions of value and of worth. To say " Fate " actually means that one is unable to come to the decision that says " Fate "; for this too is merely the process of necessity and has no reality or meaning. Fate by its very nature carries the kiss of death.

Providence

Those who have seen the dangers of analogy when it is used to limit God's creative power to the initial moment of creation have frequently become involved in another difficulty when they have tried to solve the problem by extending the time duration of God's creative power. They wished, in some way, to show that the divine initiative is not removed and to undergird the belief that God's authority still stands over everything that he has made. Any human creator has a plan that he uses as the basis of his whole work. In the case of small activities it is merely in the mind of the creator, but in large-scale projects there is a set of blueprints or a detailed scheme of work. Then the program advances in an orderly and well-planned way. This is obviously necessary in the field of human planning, and anyone who undertakes a project without sufficient planning is doomed to frustration and probable failure. It is very natural that, in the use of analogy, men imagine a detailed plan in the mind of God, a heavenly blueprint of reality, and a goal that would represent the successful completion of the project. The words that have been traditionally used and misused in theology to explain this divine activity are *providence* and *predestination*.

" Providence " is a term that points to God's providing power. The word comes from *pro* (for) and *videre* (to see), and means *foreseeing,* or able to see everything in advance, so that everything necessary will be available at the right time. This concept is very readily utilized by those who conceive of God as creating at the beginning of time. Providence then refers to the mechanical process by which everything is ordered. God not only created but at the same time foresaw the whole process of history. When used in this way it is difficult to see any difference between providence and predeterminism. There are some who claim that foreseeing is not the same as predetermining, in that foreseeing gives opportunity for free will. This is a quibbling with words. If God foresaw, he also foreordained; and even if he provided for free will, this also comes within the totality of his predetermined plan. This concept, interpreted with a strict regard for the time emphasis, makes man a puppet with only imaginary free will. It also leaves unanswered the whole question of evil and tragedy that God presumably not only foresaw but also foreordained.

The same is true of the idea of predestination, which is providence applied to the more specific sphere of the salvation of the human soul. Christians have always been convinced that salvation is not an achievement of man. He who across the years comes to a deep understanding of reality is aware that this is not something that he has created by his own power and inherent ability. Certainly he has acted, planned, and thought through the disturbing problems of the mind, he has lived through an infinite number of experiences of life that have served as the basic material in building his convictions, but he has not created the material. The experiences of life, the record of man's response to the eternal, the very concepts that he uses to examine his own response, are all there, given to him from beyond. Somehow God has acted in and through the events of life so that man, as a man in his own time, has come to this realization. Hence the concept of predestination.

This thought also becomes involved in difficulties when it is interpreted in relation to a time scheme. Eventually one is forced back to the thought that everything has been ordained from the very beginning of time and that even our own individual destiny has been determined. This cuts the nerve of human striving, and it is not true to our human experience. We believe and act as though freedom of will and decision are real. If this is merely illusion, then life itself is nothing more than a mockery.

It is important to understand that the words " providence " and " predestination " are never used in Scripture in a philosophical way. That is, they never describe life in complete detachment. They are always spoken out of a situation of involvement. They occur definitively in the letters of Paul. But when he writes of himself as chosen " before the foundation of the world " and when he speaks of God's action in bringing men and women to the place of faith in the words, " for those whom he foreknew he also predestined to be conformed to the image of his Son," he is not presenting a philosophical concept to be applied generally and objectively to the whole process of life viewed as a movement along a scientific time line. Rather, he is speaking from within the experience of faith, and his words can be understood only in the context of that relationship.

When he uses thought forms that point back to the beginning of time in claiming that God's action in choosing the Christian for faith falls into his eternal plan, he is sketching in the most graphic way he can the basic Christian experience of coming to faith. For in this experience the Christian is immediately aware of two facts. The first is that his coming to the place where he has faith is in no way his own achievement. He did not buy or catch or earn faith. Nor does a description of the stages by which he came to have faith: the experiences of life, his environment, the influence of his teachers and parents and friends — although all this description be true — completely explain the development of faith within him. In and through all of this, another power was at work, a power that was finally the essential power in this development. In and through it all, God himself acted, so that this man came to have faith. The second is that from within the experience he is aware that this action is in its very nature an activity that escapes the context of cause and effect. Although it may be given a date on a linear time scale as an event that occurs, yet in its true nature it is not solely related to the context of that time scale. " Before the foundation of the world," " foreknown," " predestined," point to the fact that this experience of faith receives its reality from beyond the context of temporality and causation. Indeed, it receives its reality from him who is the creator of the structures of temporality and causation. The words " pro " and " pre " as they occur in " providence " and " predestination " are, then, not words that refer to the context of temporality but that point to a context of importance and of precedence in value. He was speaking of priority not within the time scale but to the time scale itself.

The place where the use of the analogy of the human creator applied to God breaks down and causes real difficulty is in the use of the concept of time. The actualization of our blueprints involves time. We are creators in time and we never escape from its limitations. But God is not bound by time. God, by definition, is not bound. It is perfectly in order for us to use the concept of creativity, provided we remember the limits of our analogy. God creates in time, but he is not bound by time. There is no need for him to have a blueprint or a scheme of work that is set out along a time line. We blaspheme his nature and bind his infinite eternity to the limitations of our earthly existence when we use the analogy in this way.

It is in the present that we know God. *Now* is the ever-changing position on the linear scale of time in which we live, and although divine space time is the ground of the reality of our space time, *now* is the only occasion in which we can be aware of its reality and respond to God's presence. It may well be that our awareness and response is conditioned by remembrances from the past, either of our own experience or that of religious history. But these great events are in the present too as they grip our minds by their power and form the basis of our new response.

It is in the present that God acts. Here and now the eternal enters our time line and grasps our personalities. The Christian God is not some far-off deity who rests content in his impassivity. Nor is he the God of science who like an executive in some elevated office turns the switch that sets the machine of nature in motion. The Christian faith has always held that God participates in the affairs of this life and we know him as he acts *now*. The present is the mysterious moment in which he creates.

We have tried to channel God's creative power and to separate it from the activities of life. We have made him creative before creation and then replaced his creative power in history with a substitute system of law. The natural law controls the world of nature, which includes all the universe from its farthest reaches to its infinitesimal entities and which includes man also in so far as he participates in the natural world. The moral law defines the relationship of man with man in so far as he seems to be separate from the realm of nature and has the ability to make judgment and decision. Except for his activity in the spiritual world, this type of thought has limited God's creative activity to a point of time. Here in what seems to be a small and comparatively unimportant area of man's life, God has been permitted to wield his sovereign power.

This area of the spirit has continually caused embarrassment to man. He cannot find it; he cannot analyze it; he cannot lay hold and objectify it. Indeed, he becomes so frustrated by this concept that he declares that it does not exist, and so he replaces the vague, shadowy world of the spirit with a structure of psychiatry until it is psychoanalyzed completely out of existence.

The objective approach has proved to be most useful to man in enabling him to free himself from many imagined fetters. There was a time when the volcano displayed the anger of the god, when the earthquake, tempest, and lightning showed his fury. But we have analyzed the rumblings of the volcano to the belated bubblings of a cooling world, we have seismologized the earthquake, we have surrounded the tempest with isobars and thermographs, have dotted the cumulo-nimbus clouds with symbols of positive and negative electricity until the lightning flash is just a big spark re-establishing stability. There was a time when the great river was worshiped as a god as she nourished the fertile valley through which she flowed. But we have dammed the river and with nonchalance we draw what we need for our use. There was a time when, before a decision could be made, men would seriously and solemnly seek the advice of the gods by studying the entrails of animals. But that time has long passed. Men now rely upon the analytic method to determine the propitious time; and if they should come to a decision that they have no way of making analytically, they will casually flip a coin. Apart from a few minor and inconsequential areas the

God of the natural world had been quietly forced back and imprisoned at the beginning of time.

In the realm of morals and interpersonal relations the same objective method has been applied. It is true that there is a continual conflict between relativistic and positivistic theories of morals, but God is not considered a relevant factor. The question, Is it right? now means, Is it expedient? or How powerful is the authority that says it is right? Is it right? can mean either, Can I afford to take any other step? or Do you know if the Supreme Court has any specific ruling against it? And while moralists summon the relativistic guard for defense and the positivistic team for attack, the God who in his creativity judges right and wrong is quietly relegated to the back seat of the stands.

But we must realize again that the man who objectifies, for the time being excludes himself from immediate contact with the present. He had endeavored to set himself apart from life so that he may hold life at arm's length and examine its nature. In doing so, he has lost the immediacy of life itself.

Martin Buber expresses this truth in mythical form in *Between Man and Man,* in which he tells the story of a dream. The dream had occurred a number of times, always in a similar setting and always with the same sequence. In the course of the dream he uttered a hoarse, wordless cry from the depths of his soul. Then an answer came back in another cry that satisfied the deepest longings of his being and he realized that "Now it has happened." The last time the dream occurred the same sequence was present, but this time he realized he was waiting for the answering cry. No cry was heard. But though the distant wastes brought no audible response he was aware that the answer had come almost seeping through every pore of his body as though it had always been there.[16]

The myth underscores heavily the fact that objectification cannot be associated with the answer that relates man to the ground of his being. The movement of divine creativity cannot be objectified.

This is also implicit in all references in Scripture and elsewhere to the holiness of God. In the " tent of meeting," Moses is told " man shall not see me and live " (Ex. 33:20). He is only permitted to view, or objectify, the glory of God. His eyes, his face, his presence, his being are not the object of man. To make them such is to blaspheme the relationship of life and thus to die. Although " holy " means sacred and set apart, the set-apartness is not the separation of objectivity; it is, rather, a differentiation from all things that fall into the category of things that man may objectify.

4

The Symbol of "Creator"

Definitive Creativity

The writer in the Bible who is most filled with the concept of the creative power of God, which is implicit throughout the whole of Scripture, is Deutero-Isaiah. He writes with graphic description of this essentially creative power. God not only spreads forth the earth; he also stretches out the heavens and gives breath to people. He opens up rivers on the bare heights, and fountains in the midst of the valley. He sets the cedar, the acacia, the myrtle, and the olive in the desert, the cypress, the plane, and the pine.

His creative power is at work in the decision of men. It is he himself who defines the real. The movement of history is directed by his hand.

> Who stirred up one from the east
> whom victory meets at every step?
> He gives up nations before him,
> so that he tramples kings under foot;
> he makes them like dust with his sword,
> like driven stubble with his bow.
> He pursues them and passes on safely,
> by paths his feet have not trod.
> Who has performed and done this,
> calling the generations from the beginning?

I, the Lord, the first,
and with the last; I am He.
(Isa. 41:2-4.)

Everything in the pattern of life falls under his creative dominion. And he defines the right.

For thus says the Lord,
who created the heavens
(he is God!),
who formed the earth and made it
(he established it;
he did not create it a chaos,
he formed it to be inhabited!):
" I am the Lord, and there is no other.
I did not speak in secret,
in a land of darkness;
I did not say to the offspring of Jacob,
' Seek me in chaos.'
I the Lord speak the truth,
I declare what is right."
(Isa. 45:18-19.)

For Isaiah, deeply imbued with the mystery of life, even evil itself comes under the dominion of the creative God.

I form light and create darkness,
I make weal and create woe,
I am the Lord, who do all these things.
(Isa. 45:7.)

The person to whom Isaiah responds is not a far-off, grandly benevolent deity whose laws are the signposts of our living. He is, rather, involved in the process of history's movement and in himself defines its reality. Isaiah obviously recognizes that man can act within the context of God's creative actions, but his action is only significant if it is in line with the stream of God's creative power. Those who bind themselves to not-God or idols are doomed to nothing. God " brings princes to nought, and makes the rulers of the earth as nothing. . . . He blows upon them, and they wither, and the tempest carries them off like stubble " (Isa. 40:23-24).

> Behold, I have created the smith
> who blows the fire of coals,
> and produces a weapon for its purpose.
> I have also created the ravager to destroy.
> (Isa. 54:16.)

A thought of such depth forces us to re-evaluate any sentimental concept of the creativity of God. Isaiah goes on to define the nature of this destruction to indicate that it is not directed against those who are in tune with the divine creative will.

> No weapon that is fashioned against you shall prosper,
> and you shall confute every tongue that rises against you in judgment.
> This is the heritage of the servants of the Lord
> and their vindication from me, says the Lord.
> (Isa. 54:17.)

The divine creativity cannot be separated from its quality of judgment and destruction. That which is not in relation with the creative activity of God is by definition doomed to extinction.

In general, the Scriptures are commenting on man's relation to God within the context of this greater concept. Only occasionally does a writer step back far enough to express as best he can the ultimate relationship, as does Isaiah. In the Old Testament the writer of Proverbs develops this dimension of depth in his intense concern with Wisdom. Wisdom is a person, a power of God, and his agent in his creative work.

The Lord gives wisdom;
from his mouth come knowledge and understanding.
(Prov. 2:6.)

The Lord by wisdom founded the earth;
by understanding he established the heavens;
by his knowledge the deeps broke forth,
and the clouds drop down the dew.
(Prov. 3:19-20.)

Wisdom is the creative expression of the eternal, creating and pervading the structures of time. Though man is urged to listen to her (Prov., ch. 8) and to get wisdom (ch. 4:7), yet she can never be found or grasped by man.

Whence then comes wisdom?
And where is the place of understanding?
It is hid from the eyes of all living,
and concealed from the birds of the air.
(Job 28:20-21.)

In all this there is a concept of the creative source of reality that is intimately associated with God himself. In this way God reveals himself, consummates his plans, speaks to man. Wisdom is his outgoing word.

In the New Testament it is the Christ who is the Wisdom of God. He is the appearance of this personal eternal Wisdom in human form. John, in the opening of his Gospel, uses almost the same thought patterns as Isaiah to describe the Christ, the Word. He was with God before creation. He was the agent of God in creation and the life of man.

Paul uses the same gigantic theme in presenting the power and divinity of Christ. " He is the image of the invisible God, the first-born of all creation; for in him all things were created, . . . and in him all things hold together." (Col. 1:15-17.)

We would see God as creative in every moment of time, in and through everything that exists, in and with every event that occurs. Everything in some way participates in and is involved in the creative process of the eternal. The grandiose plan that never becomes actualized exactly as it was conceived, the idealistic scheme that creates happiness and concord, the vicious and destructive machination of the warped mind, rising out of frustration, fear, and guilt, the unconscious evil and the unrealized good, the agony of despair and the joy of achievement, the art of love and the art of hate, all these in some way are involved in the creative eternal process. The struggle of the individual to find himself and his place as he passes through succeeding stages of calmness, anxiety, discontent, and renewed endeavor, the pattern of accepting and rejecting, developing, molding, readjusting; the parental pattern of coaxing, condemning, guiding, inspiring by which young unmolded personalities are developed for good and ill, molded, twisted, warped, sharpened, purified, strengthened and diverted — developing concepts that will later flower to grandeur or be completely rejected by the adolescent struggling to assert his freedom from his past; the vigorous striving of maturity, the adult reaction to buying and selling, the struggle to make a place in the business world, to find security and fleeting happiness; the ponderings of the fact, blasphemous or beautiful; the philosopher producing critical, cynical, or creative thought; the platitudes of the pious; the circumspect life of conventionalism, orthodox, neo-orthodox, or liberal; the negating tenseness and insecurity of the nonconformist, the adjustment of the well adjusted, the neurosis of the ill adjusted, the sanity of the sane and the schizophrenia of the insane: all this is participation.

The self-assurance of the politician who molds structures of relationship that will produce new understanding or global conflicts in the years ahead; the hesitancy and uncertainty of the lover so transparent that he dreads offending; the tension of the schoolteacher who either seeks to provide opportunity of development of personality toward some goal of which he is not fully aware or vigorously molds personality to a definite pattern and sows the seeds of a future violent reaction or frustrated conformity: this, too, is participation. The ecstasy of the ball game, the joy of the honeymoon, the spontaneity of friendship, the thunder of the jet, the imbecility of the gambler, the fearfulness of the electronic brain or the electronic bomb: all this and more is circumscribed by and participates in the creative power of God.

Is there an analogy upon which we can draw to illustrate this all-pervasive quality of God's power? The most suitable analogy is probably that of the all-pervasive nature of air. Air is everywhere, unseen, supporting life, providing energy and space for action, providing oxygen for human lungs, bearing life-giving water mites in water that provide oxygen for fishy gills, in walls of brick or stone or wood providing insulation, giving carbon dioxide to trees and plants, surrounding the vacuum defining its limits. Scarcely recognized, seldom considered, and yet essential in every moment of life, air is a basic necessity for existence and creativity in our world. The analogy is again limited, for air is unconscious, mechanical, space defined and space defining; but its all-pervasive quality can stand as a symbol for the all-pervasive creativity of God. Little wonder that *rūah,* the Hebrew word for the wind of the desert, was also used for the spirit of the eternal. As all-pervasive and mysterious, as calm and gentle and yet violent and forceful, as absolutely essential as the wind of the desert was to the nomad tribe of the Hebrews, so also was the creative spirit of the eternal God who caused his sun to shine on the evil and the good and his rain to fall on the just and the unjust.

Creation and Fall

The basic concept that we form of God is that he is creator. This is a primary and enduring concept. He is creative. This is his very nature. Tillich writes: "The divine life is creative, actualizing itself in inexhaustible abundance. The divine life and the divine creativity are not different. God is creative because he is God." [17] We proceed then to speak of the originating, sustaining, and directing creativity of God in such a way that all of life is encompassed by the power of divine creativity.

It is not surprising that the opening words of the Bible are about creation. Creativity, the coming into being of newness, is life in its essential form being actualized within the structures of existence. Where does man stand in this continuing process of creativity? He is first of all created. His basic origin is out of the formless void into the stuff of existence. From this he is formed structurally. Into his frame is then breathed the breath of life.

The message of the Bible is distorted if we take this literally. Adam is man, and the story is not a fairy tale beginning with "Once upon a time." The time of the Creation is not set at 4004 B.C., as former theologians held it to be; nor at three billion years ago, as has been conjectured. This story is not a time-line story. In another sense it applies to every moment of the time line. It is the story of the continuing divine creativity. In this, man is created. He, along with the rest of creation, is a product both of the formless void from which he was created and of the powerful Spirit of God who has created him. But the original statement stands. " And God saw everything that he had made, and behold, it was very good." (Gen. 1:31.)

Continuous with the Creation story stands the Fall. The Fall does not stand apart from Creation. It is the second act of the drama. The symbolic " created out of nothing" of the creeds implies the possibility of reversion into nothing, and man stands in the tension between something and nothing, between real and the unreal. The serpent was one of God's created creatures. It is important that we see that there is no dualism here. All this occurs within the context of divine creativity, and the possibility of the Fall is all part of the process of Creation.

As the record of Creation is not time-bound, so also the story of the Fall is not to be taken as tied to " once upon a time." Creation is continually present. The creativity of God defines the present. Always with this is associated the possibility of the Fall. Here and now, whenever here and now comes into existence, is the continual possibility of the Fall.

What, then, is the nature of the Fall? It is the thesis of this book that for us the basic nature of the Fall is dominating objectification. There is within the nature of creation itself a quality of objectification, for there is identity, but it is a " dreaming innocence " type of objectification. The story of the Fall tells of eating of the tree of knowledge that would give wisdom, the opening of the eyes, and the ability to know good and evil. But " wisdom " has as much the implication of controlling intelligence as has the essential creative power of God. The opening of the eyes is something more than mere physical sight, for physical sight is already part of creation. The opening of the eyes here refers to the splitting, breaking apart, of the sight. Knowing good and evil is equally well used for differentiating between the suitable or useful and the negative or destructive. The disaster of the Fall is clearly spelled out in the Biblical story where the creature forgets its creatureliness and endeavors to be " like God." Man caught in the tension between something and nothing seeks to define himself as something; but of himself, he is not able to escape the tension. The realm that he objectifies and dominates is finally nothing. The likeness of God that man seeks to grasp is a shadow likeness without substance. It is the dimension of depth, of which man is vaguely aware and to which he is related in his state of innocence, projected onto the two-dimensional plane of existence. But the shadow projection is distorted, and man grasps at it as his relation to the depth and wears it as his cloak of divinity.

The concept of original sin and sin as separation are here bound together in one package. Man is created into a world of things. Objectification and separation are a part of its nature and a necessary element in his identity. That the structures of existence always present this possibility is the continuous nature of sin, and the fact that man is continually making this possibility an actuality is his personal and collective sin.

The judgment on sin is death. The words of the story tell Adam concerning the tree that " in the day that you eat of it you shall die " (ch. 2:17). The specious arguments of the serpent are that " you will not die. For God knows that when you eat of it your eyes will be opened, and you will be like God, knowing good and evil." The interesting thing is that both are right. Adam does not die physically on the day when he knows in shadow form the good and the evil, but whenever he employs dominating objectification he commits spiritual suicide, for he defines himself as a thing among things. He kills a relationship that holds within itself the very quality of true life.

The person who seeks to be " creative " claims that he can objectify without dominating. The painter or the sculpturer sees an object that desires to be made into a work of art. The creative writer is in touch with a situation to which he responds with the use of verbal forms, so that he creates it into a novel or a poem or a drama. The same thought can be carried through into all fields of human endeavor. It assumes that in all the actuality of the created universe there is a depth by which the man himself is grasped and to which he responds. In so far as his response is true he is truly creative. In so far as his response is distorted he fails to be related to the creative depth and defines himself out of the context of the real.

It is important to recognize here a subtle relatedness between faith and science, between involvement and objectification. It is possible to objectify and also to be grasped. A man may gaze at a picture that he recognizes as an object and yet as he gazes he may be grasped at the very center of his being. He is still aware of the object and of himself as viewing subject, but in and through it all he is involved in the primacy of relation. Out of this involvement he is created and he creates.

When the scientist regards his world, he objectifies. He recognizes both his object and himself as objectifying subject. From this point the road is divided. He may consider himself as controlling and dominating or as being involved; he may naïvely consider that he observes reality or he may be aware that the essentially real continually eludes his grasp; he may analyze and synthesize with the view to increasing his power or he may act in the hope that he will participate in the ongoing process of creation. In so far as he acts in the former of these alternatives he is remaining in the field of dominating objectification, and in so far as he acts in the context of response he opens himself to the possibility of being involved in the creative.

This assumes that there is a relatedness between that which comes into existence and the creative purpose of the divine. The Christian faith always makes this assumption. It rejects both the belief that history is purely illusory on the one hand and the philosophical contention that it is determined on the other. It would recognize that we are never fully aware of reality in so far as the essentially real is the divine that can never be objectified but is always and only in relation. We then gaze through a glass darkly; we are in the land of shadows. But for all this, everything that comes into existence has its own relation to the creative depth. There is no thing that cannot be so grasped by the depth that is implicit in its very existence that it participates in the essential actualization of the creative.

As an extreme case of this we can point to the crucifixion of Christ. Here was an event that appeared to carry all the marks of pure evil, negativity, and destruction. The surface powers of the world and its structures laid hold of him and destroyed him. But even in the event there is a definite quality of depth. Even this event when related to the depth dimension participates in essential creativity. It is an event that can be regarded as nothing or one that has the power to become something and grasp us. This event, set on the plane of history, can step out of the past with a power of presentness and be the bearer of the creative spirit. That this can happen is in fact the basis of the Christian church.

Any event, then, has the quality of depth implied within it even though it may appear to be bound to the structures of negativity. God in his threefold nature defines reality. God the Father is the depth; God the Son is the defining of the depth upon the surface, the creative appearing and the actualization of the real; and God the Spirit interprets the actuality to the surface, so that relatedness comes. And all are one. From the surface, God is the dimension of depth that maintains the surface and gives it its place and movement.

Meaninglessness and Meaning

Above all else, God is creative, continually and essentially creative. The record of Scripture is a record of, and an attempt to interpret, the movement of his creative power within the structures of time and space. But the person of Christ who is also Wisdom is of different dimensions from those observable to man. The observable dimensions are analyzable and controllable; therefore, man seeks to direct their course. He endeavors to exert his creative power. In so far as he makes these dimensions ultimate and thus defines himself to be God he crucifies the Christ, the Wisdom. The death of Jesus was actually the assertion of the ultimacy of the dimensions of this world. This assertion is finally doomed to failure, for the Christ has his being in the dimensional relation that surpasses and indeed enfolds the limited dimensions of man. So comes the resurrection, the fully real asserting its reality over against the apparent, the analyzable, the restricted reality. But in the situation in which the assertion is made the result within the structures of existence is futility and meaninglessness.

I personally and you personally are continually caught in the web of objectivity, although we are also aware in our being that this should not be so. We have become so used to holding things and people away from us and submitting them to analysis that we are unable to enter into true relationship with them. We continually strive to be in control. The day, the week, the year, is mapped out in advance on the basis of our analysis of our own past performance and the concepts we have of the movement and reaction of our environment. When unexpected events occur that expose the fact that we are not really in control we often respond with unreasoned vehemence. We feel that we have been betrayed.

The person who deceives us becomes the object of our hatred, and he who maps out a plan of life that brings to him more of this world's success becomes the object of our envy. The disasters that come, the tragic events — war, poverty, sickness, bereavement — which are never included in our plans, can bring a response of bitterness, ruthlessness, loss of confidence, and neurosis. Their unpredictability can develop within us a strenuous drive of determination that despite all things and all thing-men we are yet going to dominate and control our world, or they can so threaten us that we retire from the battle and hide in the walled fortress of our own seclusion. In either solution we still are convinced that we are winning the battle. If our new drive is thwarted or our seclusion is invaded, we either escape into neurosis or drive forth in another avenue of supposed advance. The varying attitudes of self-pity, self-centeredness, egomania, pride, and jealousy all spring from our frustration at not being able to control, or being only apparently in control.

We do, admittedly, always allow for the unpredictable, to which we give the name fortune, chance, or luck. It is the conformation of events that we did not take into consideration. This we regard as no fault of ours. We work on the basic assumption that they should not really have happened. If the chance event aids our personal scheme, we call it good luck; and if it does not, we call it bad luck.

We each one personally are caught in the web of an objectifying process and we are continually tempted by our pride to regard our objectification as life itself. But life is not bound in our schemes. It happens before them all. Life in its essential living occurs, as it were, at the prow of the boat. But all that we can do, although we are carried along by the boat, is to analyze the turning waves and gaze at the wake. Yet we are aware that we move only because the prow is breaking through that still water and that this forward point of impact is the point of creativity.

We are vaguely aware that our true destiny is to be related to the point of creativity, to be essentially related to the present. The present is the moment to which we are continually bound. Prisoners of the present, we have no voice in its coming or its going. And in this present there is no objectifying. There is only living. In the final count we are convinced that this is more real, if more mysterious, than all our activity of analyzing and controlling the present that has now gone into the past.

The word for the present is not and never can be objectivity. It is always relation.

Let us look again at the way Buber differentiates by his use of what he calls the two primary words that man speaks: I-Thou and I-It. The former is relation, the latter is experience and objectivity.

> If I face a human being as my *Thou*
> and say the primary word *I-Thou* to him,
> he is not a thing among things, and
> does not consist of things. [18]

It is, of course, always possible, indeed necessary, to objectify:

> I can take out from him the color of his
> hair or of his speech or of his
> goodness. I must continually do this.
> But each time I do this he ceases to
> be *Thou* . . .
> I can set him in a particular time and
> place; I must continually do it; but
> I set only a *He* or a *She,* that is an
> *It,* no longer my *Thou.*[19]

Objectivity is necessary in existence. But the realness of life is in the relation of I-Thou.

> So long as the heaven of *Thou* is spread out
> over me the winds of causality cower at my heels,
> and the whirlpool of fate stays its course.
>
> I do not experience the man to whom I say *Thou,*
> But I take my stand in relation to him,
> in the sanctity of the primary word . . .
>
> Even if the man to whom I say *Thou*
> is not aware of it in the midst of his experience,
> yet relation may exist.
>
> For *Thou* is more than *It* realizes.
> No deception penetrates here;
> here is the cradle of the Real Life.[20]

In this thought relation is the cradle of life and creativity.

What of the people whom we call creative? The artist, the poet, the dramatist, the business executive who is imaginatively alert, and the statesman who by his awareness and creative ability molds a people? What of the creative urges within the soul of every man that become expressed in his work, his family, and his social life? What of the ecstasy of love, the thrill of producing something of value, the enjoyment of teaching, the satisfaction of spending energy for the development of social activities that produce a sense of fulfillment?

Yes, all these people are somewhat aware of Thou. They are at least free of the structures of convention, which is an objective pattern in which men have tried to capture the real. They have all responded in some way to the call of the depth. But all at the same time seek to express this new awareness in form, and the great temptation is to stay within the structure of the new objectivity.

Many people are afraid of being open, for there is a danger in openness. Whom do you respond to as Thou? This is in one way the most " absurd " and yet the most important question that plagues the whole existentialist school. We speak of being open, we speak of responding to Thou. But who is this Thou to whom we respond? Is it possible that we respond merely to our own mirror image in our Thou? Is it possible that we respond to a Frankenstein monster liberated of our neurosis or created by society? Is it possible, and this is much more tragic, that in our openness we open ourselves to nothing? It is obviously not enough to say, " Feel free of the conventional patterns of your society," or, " Be open to the mystery of life's non-objectivity." We cannot accept that the person who frees himself from the patterns of his mores, says, " Feel free," and sets out on a rampage of lust or murder, is responding to anything other than the Thou of his own animal nature. It is probably true that the Thou of reality has at some time grasped him. He has at one time caught a glimpse of the depths of life. But he has turned away from the relation into a warped relation of his own objectifying, which he mistakenly regards as the really real.

George Bernard Shaw, as one of the most prolific and most penetrating dramatists of our age, was a man who responded to relation. As such he was vividly aware of the inadequacies of our culture and reacted strongly against the materialism of the age and the mechanistic philosophy that enslaved it. His criticism was scathing. In his own life he expressed the unconventional reaction that his writings portray. But his attempt to develop an approach that was more than mere reaction ended in failure.

He readily recognized the place of religion but fell victim of the easy and nonrelational solution of accumulating the basic concepts of all great world religions and thus failed to be grasped by the nature of a true religion. He had to fall back on some human quality as the basis of his new world. Huxley had seen it as arising out of the increasing use of the objective method. Against this Shaw rebels. His hope for salvation comes through the development of the will and he calls religion " vitalism." In *Back to Methuselah* he presents life in its maturity in the form of the Ancients who are people who have mastered the will sufficiently to live for three hundred years, to do without sleep, and to exist in continuous contemplation. By the power of the will they have a " direct sense of life " and are able to engage in the essential creative process that is self-creation. Eventually they hope to master the will completely and make themselves immortal.

This greatest of Shaw's plays, as far as its penetration if not its dramatic quality is concerned, ends as a farce. He is as much involved in the objective process as are the mechanics whom he condemns. The control of the will merely for the purpose of contemplation in order to achieve self-creation is as naïve a solution of life's fulfillment as the unconscious drive in the neo-Darwinian school.

It is significant that the most popular novelists and dramatists of our present scientific day of rapid advance in objectification all present life in tragic garb. We have been described as a rootless people, an age that has lost its sense of relation to the ground of being. We are not sure if anything has any meaning any more. We see ourselves as extremely creative and point with an uncertain pride to the amazing changes that we have achieved in the world of nature and man during the last two centuries, but the pride remains uncertain and the pointing finger trembles because we are not sure if we have created something or nothing. If the creativity of God defines the real, then he is reality and in our linear time that which conforms to his creative purpose is real and that which does not conform is unreal and futile. Man has his freedom and his creative ability. It is, therefore, entirely possible that his creative expression may be completely out of step with the creative purpose of God and be meaningless.

The fear that our life itself may be irrelevant dominates the thought of many modern novels and plays, particularly those arising from the existentialist school. This is one of the themes of Beckett's *Waiting for Godot.* This two-act play has only one dominant goal — the appearance of Godot, who is never described and who never appears. The movement of the play is the completely irrelevant antics of two tramps who are waiting for Godot. They begin to question the actuality of Godot and even to doubt the fact that they are there. " You do see me, don't you? " cries one of Beckett's heroes to Godot's angelic messengers. " You're sure you saw me; you won't come and tell me tomorrow that you never saw me!"[21] Out of all the confusion and buffoonery, the hysteria and nightmare, which one realizes is not only the quality of these two tramps but, to Beckett's cynical mind, a comment on the cosmic loneliness and confusion of the modern soul, only one thing is clear: they are waiting for Godot. If he comes, they will know if their life is relevant or not.

Is the laugh of life one of the ringing joy of fulfillment or is it merely a bray of hollow mockery echoing down the ravines of meaninglessness? This is a realistic and significant question that is being enunciated in our time. We want to know what is real and relevant and meaningful, and we want to know what is superfluous, absurd, irrelevant, and meaningless. And this is an urgent question. In these days the whole range of experience is being called into question. We have within our power the mysterious ability of creativity; indeed, we cannot escape creating in time. But the fear dwells within us that, when we have finished our creating, life or history or God may look at our creation and laugh with mocking judgment: "You have created a monstrosity. You have created a bubble of meaninglessness utterly irrelevant."

For Faulkner, "du Homme" becomes anglicized to "Doom," and in this the theme of modern letters is spelled out. However exciting may be the advance in the limited field of technology, for the dramatist and the poet opening himself to the breathing of human life the experience is one of loneliness and doom, estrangement and fear. T. S. Eliot holds the mirror to our age in:

> We are the hollow men
> We are the stuffed men
> Leaning together.
> Headpiece filled with straw. Alas!

Our dried voices, when
We whisper together
Are quiet and meaningless
As wind in dried grass
Or rats' feet over broken glass
In our dry cellar.[22]

Man lives in an atmosphere of dis-ease. There is a chronic sickness that affects him, and the sickness is part of the givenness of his life. He must objectify to live. He must analyze the situation in which he finds himself in order to make plans for the future. He continually objectifies the world in which he lives, separating its materials and using their power. He objectifies the people whom he meets so that he may have some organized relationship with them. But he is aware that as he objectifies he destroys. That which he subjects to the penetrating ray of his analyzing reason no longer comes to meet him. He does not encounter it, for it is dead. It belongs to the past. Man has this wonderful power of understanding, but he can only bring it to bear on the past that has already gone never to return.

He takes great pride, and yet has a twinge of uneasiness, in the fact that he can control what he objectifies and make it his slave. He works long at the structure of nature and finally comes through with an understanding of some of its power; he continually investigates the nature of the human mind and promptly incorporates his findings into an educational system by which he can control the development and reaction of the mind.

All this can be good. But always the danger is that he will not only understand but also dominate and misuse. He lords it over his analyzed object and thinks that he is god. And here comes the vicious nature of his disease. As he objectifies, dominates, and reigns he finds that although he wants to be in relationship, he is actually king of things with which he can have no relationship. Although he appears the divine orderer as he views his creations, he finds that he is actually god of a dead world of his own objectifying. Man, with his power of standing apart, objectifying, and dominating even his own kind, is always in danger of defining himself as a thing-man and of condemning himself to the doom of things. But the life that is the essential quality of man in the now is never objectified. It is lived. Objectification, if it comes, comes later, after the now has become then. It is an element in the deadening process of falling into the past. It is not there in the life of now.

In the structures of time and space this is the nature of man's predicament. His main conscious activity is related to the dead past even when he is endeavoring to apply this to the future. But at the same time his main and only living activity is his response to the now that encounters him in every moment of time. How can man be freed from this predicament? How can he be cured of this sickness? Some cure must be provided if he is not to be destroyed in his self-constructed tomb of thingness.

The Christian faith sees the cure in the Christ. He is the life that gives reality to the present, and it is his livingness that we destroy in the deadening process of objectivity. And he has solved the predicament and provided the cure by submitting himself to the limitations of finitude and temporality. In the life of Jesus we see nonobjectifiable life placing Jesus in the situation where deadening objectification automatically occurs and the temptation to thingness is continually present.

Men made Jesus a thing. They were incapable of remaining in relationship or presentness with him, so they followed their traditional procedure of relegating him to the past, analyzing and dominating and turning him into a thing. Having done this, it was an easy step to give him the doom of thingness and crucify him.

The amazing message of the resurrection is that life is victorious over thingness, that the nonobjectifiable is more powerful than objectivity. The creative power of life, the wisdom and the word of the creating God, is of greater dimensions than existence and cannot finally be captured in its structures or death doomed by its process of objectivity. The conviction of the Christian church is that it is in relation with this *Thou* that man is related to reality and his energetic striving is truly creative. *Thou* was regarded as a *him,* and *It* was then destroyed. But *Thou* demonstrated power to overcome the structures of the objective. In relation to the *Thou* is the source of the creative.

All this is included in John's description of Christ as the word of God. " All things were made through him, and without him was not anything made that was made." (John 1:3.) Paul expounds the same theme in " In him all things were created, . . . and in him all things hold together " (Col. 1:16-17). Christ is the outgoing creative word of God, the extension of God's personality into the world.

In this thought God creates the now that defines the present, and the creative power of God is continually active in the present. All that creates in thought or word or act receives its permission and its power from the creative Christ of God. The energy of nature or of man is not seen as energy in and of its own right but deriving its whole existence from the creative Christ.

Within his own limits man has his freedom. The creative power within him may be directed as he wills, with this proviso, that if what he wills is out of the context of the creative will of God, his act and achievement will be meaningless and will condemn to meaninglessness all those who are involved in it.

The great temptation is that man decides that his energy is his own, his act is his own, and his achievement is his own. He defines the real. This blasphemous and common attitude carries within it the germs of alienation, guilt, and frustration. This is the meaning of the Fall and of the doctrine of original sin. Man is continually tempted to define himself as God.

The Christian faith sees the coming to understanding of man of his predicament as the work of the Spirit of God. It is not by his own creative act that man comes to that relationship with the creative Christ which is called faith. It is by the power of God himself by his Spirit.

In the act of faith as a Christian, man recognizes that he is not God. He realizes that the continual temptation is to define himself as God. He knows that God has involved himself in this blasphemy and has risen above it, that he continually involves himself in it and rises victorious. With this awareness man recognizes that he is not God and so relates himself to God through faith in Christ. He acknowledges that his energy — mental, spiritual, physical — is from the creative power of God and his activities are directed by this acknowledgment. He prays for forgiveness because he succumbs continually to the temptation to deify himself and to reject the Christ, and he is aware that this act of self-deification carries the doom of death.

Human Creativity

The relation of the Christian man to the cultural structure, activities, and opportunities of his age is an ambiguous one. On the one hand, he will regard none of them as the final context to be elevated to deity; and on the other, he will immerse himself in them, realizing that they are for him the outward conformation of the true and hidden context in which his life has meaning. His culture is the historical context in which his life must be lived, and he will seek to live it to the full. But he will never see his ultimate relation as being to that culture.

To all outward appearances he will strive to be successful, but his striving will in no way make success his context and his god. If his talents and training have led him to be a teacher, he will strive to be the best teacher that he can be. If he is a doctor, a farmer, a lawyer, a parent, a businessman, a politician, a laborer, a social worker, a scientist, an engineer, or a psychiatrist, he will do all that he can to be successful in his field.

He will enter into the activities of his culture with interest and enthusiasm, realizing that these are in some way related to the creative context that is God himself. His critical faculty will remain alert because he is aware of the constant temptation to deify any aspect of his cultural scene and he will not be willing to apply the adjective " eternal " to any structure within society nor to give it his ultimate allegiance. Nevertheless, he will also be aware that the creative activities of men, although often misdirected, often but partially true, and sometimes completely misinformed, are yet for him, in his time, aspects of the creative activity of the divine.

He is likely to classify cultural activity in three broad

categories: positive creativity; rebellious creativity; and idolatrous creativity, or creativity that has been directed into superficial and idolatrous actions.

Positive creativity will be activity that either relates man more closely to his true context, enables him to express that relationship more effectively in life, or is itself the expression of a creative spirit that contributes to these other two. The first would be activity that is religious in nature, especially the activity of true worship, but would also include experiences that are artistic or existential in such a way that they reveal to man his true nature and dependence. The church in its true life is positively creative in that it is the organization in society that provides the occasion for man to be set in his true context. So, too, works of art that arise out of the awareness of this context of life can be powerful in their ability to show man his true self, and experiences of life that reveal its depth will be classified as positive creativity. The elation of spirit that comes through music, the sense of involvement and profound response that comes in high drama or in viewing a work of art, the dedication that is summoned forth in a situation of great challenge, the commitment that is involved in voluntary un-self-conscious sacrifice, and the ecstasy of love are all placed in this category.

This is a broad category. Under positive creativity we also place all those efforts of the creative spirit of man to mold his environment, to free himself from bondage of details, and to create situations in which he can live more fully. All cultural activities, educational programs, scientific invention and processing, political activity, study, and change in the structures of society and of institutions — all these, from world scale down to the situation of personal counseling and planning, are seen as creative activity that is positive.

As a special group come those activities of man which we most readily call creative: the painting or sculpturing of a work of art; the composing of an overture; the writing of a book, a novel, or a play; the ability to produce new thoughts, creative conversation or decoration or buildings. Often people who engage in such activity appear to be more sensitively aware of the context in which their life has meaning even though this may place them in conflict with the particular situation of their time. Many of these persons have been so sensitive to the true context of life, although often unconsciously, that they have been unable to remain in the cultural context in which they find themselves. Creative thinkers, statesmen, writers, artists, inventors, have often found themselves condemned by their culture to death or have sought escape in suicide. Their productions are always colored by the environment of their times, but as we honor them we in effect recognize the relation that they had with the meaningful context of life.

While positive creativity may be recognized as directly associated with the true context of life, the role of rebellious creativity is more difficult to evaluate. On the surface it seems so condemnatory that it is often classified as against life, or anti-God. The most obvious example of this type of creativity is the vigorous thrust of the early Christian community. So directly were these early Christians related to the true context of life that their activities appeared to be in direct rebellion to the context of the culture in which they lived. By the Roman authorities they were condemned as atheistic, immoral, cannibalistic, and hostile to culture: atheistic, because they refused to worship the

Roman gods; immoral, because they called one another brother or sister and participated in the love feast; cannibalistic, because of the mysterious hidden rite of partaking of the body and blood; and hostile to culture, because they would not participate in the cultural activities of their day.

This illustration must force us to pause before we classify the rebel as an atheist. It is always possible that he is much more closely related to the real context of life than the self-contained culture against which he rebels.

From the prophet Amos down to Jean-Paul Sartre there have been countless rebels who have done nothing more than denounce and condemn. As such, their rebellion has never had anything significant to contribute in redirection. From time to time the rebellion has been so critical of its cultural context that it has attacked those aspects which have been most deified, and the rebel has been exterminated.

Nevertheless, the rebel is creative. In his reaction against social structures he is rejecting their actual or inherent deification, which is always present. It would obviously be possible to differentiate between types of rebellious creativity. Some rebels are so completely negative in their denunciation that they succeed in destroying the deified context without providing any significant context in which life can be lived. When the old idols die with violence new idols readily take their place.

He who rebels against his cultural context on the basis of some deeper and more significant context is generally able to provide guidance even though his attack may appear to be mainly destructive and negative.

Whatever differentiation may be made, it is to be remembered that rebellious creativity is creativity. Its energy derives from the creative context of life.

Superficial creativity may be applied as a concept to all activity that is not concerned significantly with the depth of life. Within this the majority of our actions and plans would seem to fall. Yet the creative thrust, no matter how trivial may be its application, can never be completely separated from its source, and from the surface it is always possible to break through to the implied depth. It is also apparent that man can become enamored with trivial creativity and become its slave, whether it be an endless round of reinvesting in the stock market or being correct at coffee parties or turning the right screw at the right time or performing the routine of the office or classroom or household.

Idolatrous creativity occurs whenever the individual becomes ultimately bound to an aspect of existence. This is equally true of the Bohemian who dedicates himself to frolic for frolic's sake, of the prim housewife for whom cleanliness is prior to godliness, of the financier who genuflects before the almighty dollar, of the religious bigot who binds himself to the law and kills the spirit of life. Idolatrous creativity is creativity. It involves energy, activity, planning. But in the process, man's spirit is cramped into the area of his worship, and like Procrustes' guest, his life ebbs away within the confines of his prison bed.

5

Absurdity and Reason

We are creatures who are committed to being reasonable. Not that everything we do is reasonable; but when an event occurs, we are convinced that we can give the reasons for it. We set life and its processes within the unalterable framework of cause and effect. The tragic error arises when mankind makes the assumption that the law of cause and effect that he uses to analyze the past can also be transferred without reservation to the future. We fail to realize that when we analyze the past, an essential element has already evaporated away. That element is life. It is no longer there. Only the use of imagination can inject a semblance of life into the already dead event. And to take the structures of the past, in which *rigor mortis* has already taken place, and to transfer them to the future is to bypass life, to discount the element of creativity, and to define existence in the cold structures of causality. To do this is to murder life.

But life will not die. Life lives. In those eras of man's history when reason has become the yardstick of life, there has come an inevitable rebellion against its stringent bondage. The Greek philosophers lifted the standard high, but it was torn down in a series of intercity wars. The Romans became impregnated with stale thought, and the Empire fell. Fate ruled destiny, and destiny destroyed the bondage of fate. Medieval philosophy reached its peak in Thomas Aquinas, who used not only the thought patterns of Christian theology but also the rationality of Aristotle, and from that peak it crumbled to its ruin. The deists took up the cry of living according to the nature of things, and the vital forces of the industrial revolution destroyed this reasonable world. Life will never be condemned to death, and repeatedly asserts its sovereignty over all the cold objectification of reason.

In the Western world the industrial revolution enabled man to break through a barrier that had been imprisoning him for centuries. With the principle of causality in his hand directed against the things of the world he set out on a march of conquest. The same rational principle was directed against the structures of his society and with the fall of the barriers in the streets of Paris, the beginning of a long series of political rebellions, man became free—free, tragically free; free to be caught in the paralyzing ray of his own causality. First he was a " hand," merely a tool in the machine process. Then, with the theory of evolution he found his creativity stripped from him, and he was defined as an animal functioning according to the set laws of his species. Then, in his struggle to maintain at least a minimum of privacy that could be called human he sought refuge in the quiet insanity of convention.

For Western man and for the world the twentieth century is the era of rebellion. Man cannot endure being classified as a machine; he cannot believe that he is merely an animal. So the cry goes out to reject the bitter domination of causality, to step out of the objectification to cause and effect, and to be committed. " Blood and soil," cried the Nazis as they peeled back the superficial layers of twentieth-century life. " Dedicate yourself to the state," is the appeal of communism. " Believe in democracy, exercise your freedom," has become the call of the Western world. But democracy is vaguely defined, and often freedom means only freedom to live in the prescribed pattern and to cheat at the personality tests that will determine one's future.

The whole world is in rebellion against the deadening principle of causality as it is applied to man. He has created the machine and has set his strength against it. But in the battle between man and the machine the final issue is not yet decided.

Poets, artists, writers, in starting to peel back the layers of stereotype thought, have come through with the concept that life is absurd.

After describing the way in which he came to realize that he was " superfluous to all eternity," Sartre writes:

> Absurdity was not an idea in my head nor the sound of a voice, it was this long, dead, wooden snake curled up at my feet, snake or claw or talon, it was the same. Without formulating anything I knew that I had at last found the clue to my existence, to my nausea, to my life. And indeed anything I have ever grasped since that moment comes back to the fundamental absurdity.[23]

The place of the Absurd is a perfectly logical place for mid-twentieth-century man to reach. He is the inheritor of a cultural attitude which assumes that everything can be explained in scientific terms of causality and that progress can be achieved by the more thorough application of scientific analysis and synthesis. He assumes that life is basically defined in terms of reason.

Here is the blasphemy of modern man. He has become so proud of the tools with which he has managed to understand something of his world that he has assumed that those tools define the real. He has become so enamored with his own ability to create and mold across the whole pattern of life from space rockets to sales techniques that he has tricked himself into believing that he is the creator. He is the molder of history. When he does this he is involved in a farce that would be humorous if it were not so pathetic.

Man has assumed that life is rational, that it fits the rules that he has established or can establish with his reason. But when life appears to break out of the basic rules that he has established he declares that life is absurd. This is a normal, natural, and correct rational analysis. What is not rational is absurd. Here are examples that demonstrate its absurdity. And examples can be given *ad nauseam*.

There is really no need to belabor the point that life is absurd. The point has effectively been made. All that it means is that the basic assumption that life is rational is not true. Life is no longer absurd when the basic assumption of the complete rationality of life has been discarded.

There is still a place for reason. It is a tool that we use to analyze and evaluate. But it is no longer the only tool. Even the amateur carpenter who is using a screw driver to tighten a screw will discard it without emotion when he wants to hammer a nail. And he will discard both when he wants to sit on the chair that he is constructing. In chair construction there is the screw-driverable and the non-screw-driverable, so in life there is the rational and the nonrational; and we may call the nonrational absurd, if we desire; but we should strip this word of all the overtones of vehement rebellion. It need not have emotional content, for it is a word, and words of themselves are rational. "Absurd" is merely the rational word that defines the nonrational.

But the word "absurd" is filled with implications of negativity and darkness and threat. It is a word that seems to have power to destroy the very structures of our philosophy, and we fight against it with crusading zeal. We have given it this power only because we have defined life as being in the context of the rational, and thus automatically defined absurd as being the context of not-life, or death. " Absurd," in itself, does not have this power. We ourselves invest it with this power. And we invest it with this power only because we have tried to limit life to the rational.

The same is true of the concept of " Nothing " that haunts the minds of existentialist philosophers and, as nihilism, pervades the spirits of many people in the world today. If we have been raised on the assumption that life is something, and that something is defined in terms of possessions materialistically, happiness experientially, justice politically, and success socially, and if life does not actually provide us with any of these things, then the conclusion is that life is not something; that actually and logically it is nothing.

It is apparent that our century has experienced a profound shock in discovering itself. By rational and logical means that they asumed were accurate, men painted a prognostic picture of this century in brilliantly satisfying colors. With the great development of man's technological and rational ability, his increasing understanding of his own nature and his world, there was no reason why the twentieth century should not be the long-awaited era of peace, prosperity, and good will on a world scale. The twentieth century was to be something for which men had waited.

The difference between the potential and the actual is fantastic and hellish. The something expected has not come, and man in despair calls his life Nothing. Nothingness has become a central point in the philosophy of despair that permeates our age even outside the countries that have been ravaged by war. Heinemann sums up the situation thus, when he describes " an important and most revealing event in the spiritual history of our time ":

> Whereas former ages, having discovered the transcendent God, were longing to see how he could become immanent in man and the world, our generation, believing that it has discovered transcendent Nothingness, is interested in seeing it descend into the world and into the hearts of men. Or to put it more bluntly, the superworldly devil, having lost his transcendent realm, comes down to earth making a hell of it.[24]

If this is a true analysis, then not only has man been shocked by the nonfulfillment of his dream of success and achievement, he has actually rejected his supposed deity and has turned to worship at the throne of Nothing. The adoration of an expected Something has been exchanged for involvement in the God of Nothing.

This is not surprising. The expectation was described in vague terms and in categories that had no boundaries. The something expected was an era of wealth, possessions, success, fulfillment. But these terms can never be clearly defined. No matter where you stand on the ladder of wealth or success, it is always possible to visualize being much more wealthy and much more successful. Man begins to realize that he can never be successful in a final way, and logically asserts that he is not successful; in fact, he is a failure.

The desire man has to have black or white definitions is a curse. He sets himself a goal of happiness, but when he comes to the place where he expected to attain the goal and he does not find exactly what he had expected he throws his hands up in despair and cries that he is unhappy. Logically he is right. He was striving for happiness, but he did not achieve exactly what he had expected. If what he expected was called happiness, then he did not attain it. Therefore he attained unhappiness.

This is the tragedy of the perfectionist. He lives on the assumption that he can attain perfection in all areas of life. But he is doomed to disappointment. Not only is he liable to fail to achieve perfection in this or that specific project, but time continually works against him. For perfection somehow carries the thought of permanence. That which is perfect should be perfect for all time. But nothing stands in that category. Ideas change; policies are remolded to meet a new need. The garden that appears perfect today will be filled with new weeds by next week. The perfectionist is doomed to disappointment and frustration. He can eventually come to the conclusion that the Nothing is perfect, and worship at the Shrine of the Absurd.

As a corollary of the prejudiced assertion that life is rational, we have the theological concept of God as Mind. He is the Master Mind, coldly intellectual as he performs his duty of analyzing, evaluating, and synthesizing the pattern of this universe of events. Of course, if God is Mind, the creator of life that is rational, then the Absurd or the nonrational is anti-God and anti-life. The Absurd then is hell and death. If God is Mind, then belief is merely intellectual acceptance of certain scientific formulas of his nature, and salvation is immersion in the processes of reason.

This intense preoccupation with life as reason and the definition of God as Mind has placed man in a prison house from which he must at some time escape. As the child who has been brought up in a coldly calculating environment under the limiting bondage of dominating parents must assert his freedom and rebel if he is to be himself, so man rebels against the limits that cramp his being and shackle his spirit. In this rebellion it is useless to spend time in endless controversy between the rational and the absurd, and those who spend their energies worshiping at the shrine of Nothing and proving that life is absurd are committing as fatal and as biased an error as their frantic opponents who still try to demonstrate that life is rational and that God is Something.

The place for action now, if we desire life's meaning, is to enter into life beyond the categories of rational and absurd, beyond the ambiguity of Something and Nothing. Life is actually the *sine qua non* of forming the categories of the rational and the nonrational, of striving unsuccessfully for an ill-defined Something, and of forming the bitter conclusion that it is actually Nothing that life includes.

The agony of our time arises from the conviction that God is not concerned; that we are doomed in our suffering, finitude, and death without any appeal. By using the multipurpose tool of reason, man has sought to create a world structure in which he is god, the creator and controller of destiny. Technologically he is god of his own created machine. Politically and in mass he is god of the individual in the mass. Truth, rational truth, and justice have been elevated above divinity; and man, elevating himself with them, looks down on God. Working under the great arc lamp of reason, man the surgeon has wielded the scalpel of logic to cut away the diseased flesh of divinity in the concepts of the human mind.

The whole idea of the divine has been brought into critical scrutiny by the free thinkers of the past few centuries. Jesus of Nazareth has been lifted out of the context of Hebrew thought and the significance of the Christ has been lost. He becomes the great example on some moral stage, but the lines are blurred because the moral stage of the first century has a completely different context from our modern life. Or he becomes an ignorant simpleton who, because of naïveté, is not able to understand the political pressures of his day or to act significantly within its structures. In any case the Christ is firmly captured within the human scene and loses any claim he might have to divinity. When this step has been taken, all hope that man might have that God is concerned has been lost. God becomes simply creator, distant, unimpassioned creator, the unconcerned, objective architect whose created structure is in a perpetual state of unbalance. And he leaves it that way. He is not concerned.

Man, one element in this created structure, struggles to establish himself and to find meaning, but he is continually beaten down. His body is disease-ridden; his mind is distorted; his society is sick. No matter how sincerely he strives for the good, he is eventually and always placed in the prisoner's cage and condemned to die. The sentence is carried out and there is never a reprieve. Once the Christ has been completely equated with the human predicament and defined as man, his record stands as the perfectly typical example of God's vicious dealing with his creature. The perfect man struggles through life endeavoring to relate himself to God, but the ears of God are stopped and the doors of heaven are closed. He strives for the good, but the forces of evil join together in a vigorous thrust and he dies, young and in agony.

How can God allow this to happen? The answer for him who has stripped the Christ of his divinity can only be: because this is the vicious nature of God. The Creator God has really no sense of justice, no understanding, no compassion. He is not concerned. It is an easy step from this point to assail the citadel of God himself. Man, in his existence, has developed concepts that tower far beyond the unjust, ignorant, hard God of creation by which he dethrones Him. The end is reached and Nietzsche can declare to the accompaniment of great applause that " God is dead."

But then man is trapped into the deification of his own rational concepts, and the result is the cultural disaster of the twentieth century. The deification of his own concepts of justice forced him to regard his own legal pronouncements as ultimate truth. Whoever does not conform is then sentenced to the ultimate punishment of death. Proud man defines his understanding as final reality and arrogantly destroys all those who do not accept his dictates. Mass man becomes the refiner of justice and truth and our century reels under the blows of the hammer that forges the chains of bondage.

This is a tragic position for a civilization that has so much of the Christian heritage upon which to draw. Yet this is the place that religion itself will always reach if it defines God in the Old Testament symbols of justice and wrath. The temptation for religion has always been to define rules that define God's action in this world. " Do good and God will bless you," with the implication that it will be with material blessing and this-worldly happiness, is a maxim that automatically follows from this temptation. The maxim is blasphemously superficial. The Christian should always be wary of accepting its specious reasoning by recalling that He whom they called sinless suffered poverty, homelessness, hatred, and was soon eliminated.

If there is any meaning in the gospel story, it is definitely not to be found in a reduplication of mediocre bourgeois moralism. The central message is ontological, concerned with being, relating man to the source of his life and with the ground of his being. In an incidental way it concerns his relatedness within this life and hence with the area that we call morals; but this is always secondarily and derivatively. To make it primary is to distort the message, blaspheme the Christ, damn man to superficial bondage, and, as Paul saw clearly, to condemn him to death.

Side by side with this devaluation of the divinity of Christ goes the developing materialistic philosophy of our era. With the Creator God far off and unconcerned the only reality available to man is his own sphere, the materials of his world, his own impulses, and the pattern that he establishes upon the plane of time that he calls history. Materialism directs its passion and pledges its commitment to these. It sees only this world and its structure, and in and from this world it expects salvation.

Here is the source of utopian optimism in scientific and dialectical materialism. Scientific materialism gives itself the limited task of analyzing the structures of this world in order to produce a new synthesis. Dialectical materialism engages in the much vaster task of analyzing and manipulating the structures of history in order to produce the ideal state. Materialism assumes that this world and its history are real and goes on to affirm that in fact they are the only reality. We see this trend of thought as a Christian heresy, closely associated with the heresy that denies divinity to Christ. Both are superficial because they have denied their depth. The assertion that this world and its history are real without any recognition of depth is a fantastic assertion of blind faith and infantile courage. As a purely gratuitous assumption it is continually threatened by its own discoveries. If this world is man's only reality, he will give himself with passion to its study. As we have seen, he seeks to span its sweep from the infinitesimal to the infinite and finally is forced to define himself as a " temporary chemical episode on the life of one of the minor planets." The history that he seeks to manipulate constantly eludes his control, so that in our time he who seeks to dominate and control history is usually eliminated in a purge inherent within the history that he has sought to manipulate.

Even modern man busying himself with the superficialities of his existence cannot escape the depth. Though he deny its presence, he is automatically involved. On the one side, it is because of the depth that he is even able to define his universe and history, and limits himself to the superficial; and on the other, he is encountered by the depth as it penetrates the surface of history in the form of judgment.

Camus, in *The Rebel,* traces the biography of Western civilization during recent centuries in terms of rebellion that he declares to be " the very movement of life." But he sees the present stage of rebellion as reaching stagnation.

> Immediately rebellion, forgetful of its generous origins, allows itself to be contaminated by resentment; it denies life, dashes toward destruction, and raises up the grimacing cohorts of petty rebels, embryo slaves all of them, who end by offering themselves for sale today, in the market places of Europe, to no matter what form of servitude. It is no longer revolution or rebellion but rancor, malice, and tyranny.[25]

The stage to which man has advanced in his modern manipulation of society is tragic. In the name of nobility he has denied the noble dimension of depth and condemned himself to servitude and destruction. Camus, significantly among the " atheistic " existentialists, was aware of the depth. He saw the tragedy of modern man and he sought to limit his pride and arrogance. In his conclusion he gives as the " only original rule of life today " as " to learn to live and to die, and, in order to be a man, to refuse to be a god." [26]

But his solution carries no cry of hope except in the dream quality of his poetic prose. He appeals to the Spartan existence, daring thought, and the recognition of all men as brothers.

> Each tells the others he is not God; this is the end of romanticism. At this moment when each of us must fit an arrow to his bow and enter the lists anew, to reconquer, within history and in spite of it, that which he owns already, the thin yield of his fields, the brief love of this earth, at this moment when at last a man is born, it is time to forsake our age and its adolescent furies. The bow bends; the wood complains. At the moment of supreme tension, there will leap into flight an answering arrow, a shaft that is inflexible and free.[27]

With this, Camus remains within the encampment of the romantics. This telling of one another that we are not God is merely a mouthing of meaningless words unless we give recognition to God. It is a blind nodding to the depth. For it is by our striving, by our manipulative action in the world and history, that we will bring the fairy-tale solution of freedom, justice, and truth.

The significant contribution that the whole existentialist school has to make to our times is its clear analysis of our estrangement, of our despair, of our superfluity in our present predicament. In our arrogance and the neurotic thrill of manipulation we have defined ourselves out of the context of reality. The existentialist cry is a cry from the prison house of man's own making, a cry of despair, for he knows he should be free. It is the agonizing of the crucified who has driven the nails into his own cross, condemned himself to death, and yet is vaguely aware that he is born to live.

Camus's solution is a very tentative first step, and its first clause is understandably expressed in the negative. " Each tells the other that he is not God." This faces boldly the prevalent blasphemy of our time when we have assumed that we are God. But the immediate question is, If we are not God, who is God? Is God God? If so, what is his will and the nature of his being? This is a difficult question for the writers of our time who alternately deal with the whole religious question either with a sledge hammer or with kid gloves. Yet the question must be asked.

It is not sufficient to say that the solution of our modern problems is to tell one another that we are not God and then fit an arrow into our bow. This is true, but it is only the beginning. Numerous writers are quick to provide a negative answer. God is not man. He is not the blind creator. He is not a personal God. He is not a mechanical God. He is not concerned. He is not distant. It is amazing the number of writers who are anxious to tell you what God is not. The only general implication that one can take from their writings — and this is an implication that is rarely even hinted — is that God is. This is an amazing implication. So much time is spent in destroying man's concept of God that it is very possible for the reader to lose the grandeur of this affirmation in the tangled forest vines of imprecation and atheism. But the eventual conclusion from such heaping of condemnation on this or that God is the final implication that God *is*. Whatever God is not, he is. We can be instructed by the continual negation of modern philosophers to be aware of the holy ground on which we stand and of the fact that, because it is holy ground, no one can rush in with an easy explanation. But we must not be misled by their continual hesitancy and lack of confidence into the conviction that all that can be said of God is, finally, nothing.

The Christian conviction is that God is and that he reveals himself to man — that he is involved in the events of history and the process of time in such a way that he defines the real. He is concerned. This word comes from a French root that means "mixing together." When we say that God is concerned, we mean much more than that he is interested in our world. We are actually pointing to a relationship that is intimate. To say that God is concerned means that God is involved within the events of life, from the infinite to the infinitesimal, from the cosmic to the personal.

The Christian sees the eternal wisdom and the power of God active within the structures of existence and recognizes that Jesus as the Christ participates in the ambiguities with which life is filled. It does not see him as personally participating in the Fall; this is the central message of the temptation scenes in the gospel story in which he refuses to take the place of God within the structures of existence. But it sees him as being submissive to those estranging limitations which come as a result of the Fall. In the process of his life he is misunderstood and condemned; he is made a tool of the objective process of politics and religion; he is a prisoner of the categories of human temporality and finitude; he participates both in the highest experience in the transfiguration, and in the lowest form of ignominy in condemnation, suffering, and death.

6

The Symbol of "Concern"

All the elements of living that we can use to indicate to ourselves that God is also serve to indicate that he is concerned.

The mere fact of existence can serve as evidence that God is concerned. At a very early age and from time to time throughout his life, no matter how much he may become encumbered by the very mechanics of living, a man asks himself why he is here, why the world is as it is, and why he is involved in it as he is at the particular time and place that he is. To realize that I am I, and that no one else can ever be that I for me, is a deeply moving experience. Mankind as a whole may not actually enunciate the question, "Why was I ever born? Why did I, of all people, come forth into existence at this time and at this place to face these particular problems?" Yet men by their very living, if they continue living, are saying, "There is a reason and a purpose." No matter how rudimentary may be their theology, they are implying that in some way the power behind all creation is concerned.

I would assert this quietly but firmly against all so-called agnostics and atheists who claim that they have no place for God and certainly would never acknowledge that he is concerned. The word "chance," which they use to describe why they are here, is a meaningless word and has relevance only when we use it to state that we do not understand how certain things or events happen to be related. The word " chance " is merely a confession of ignorance. If we take its common usage of indicating that there is no actual relatedness and apply it to the very structure of being, then we spell our life in terms of meaninglessness. If this is really believed, and obviously there is no reason to believe it if believing it is meaningless, then the individual concerned would automatically slowly cease to exist or more abruptly jump off a bridge. The mere fact that he continues to be with us is proof that he does not believe what he says. If he should claim that the only reason why he remains is that it is more pleasant than departing, this is quiet indication that the God who is concerned has more ways of indicating his presence than by mere logic.

The same line of reasoning can obviously be followed by asking questions about the structure of a world that provides for our needs and the orderliness of the universe in which we live. In these cases, to quote such philosophical and scientific theories as the survival of the fittest and the amazing ability of the human being's adjustment is merely to beg the question. For the ability to adjust is as much of the givenness of the situation as the fact of change. They are both part and parcel of the same structure of reality and both arise from the same creative source.

To be alive and to remain alive is to acknowledge that God is and that he is concerned. This does not in any way indicate the nature of his concern, and it only implies in a very dim and nebulous way that he is concerned with this personality I call " I." As a matter of fact, there are many factors within life that would lead me as an individual seriously to question whether he is concerned with me at all. I am aware that my life may be brought to an end at any moment in an automobile accident for which I am in no way responsible; that I may be destroyed by a disease or a disaster over which I have no control; or that I may be exterminated in a war for which I seem to have no responsibility. I am aware that my business may suffer a serious reverse that will destroy all my fondest hopes and dreams, and that the reversal may arise either from my own lack of understanding or from a cultural movement completely beyond my control. And whenever such events occur they seem to shout: " Meaninglessness "; " God is not concerned "; " God is dead "; " There is no God "; " Life has no purpose or relatedness or meaning."

Within existence itself the most obvious immediate challenge to the belief in a concerned God is the fact of death. There comes a time when we cease to be, when we give up the space that has been solely occupied by this I, when we relinquish to others all that we have accumulated, and, as far as this world is concerned, we cease to be. Death is the final expression of all the anxieties, fears, frustrations, failures, sufferings, and defeats that we experience in this life. It is the last rapier thrust of nonbeing. Yet it is a significant fact that in general, although death is always and in every moment a possibility for us, we continually accept life. We cannot imagine our name in the obituary column, though we know it will certainly appear there, and in the most dire sickness we usually strive for life even though death appears to be the most normal conclusion.

It is apparent that life, and existence itself, is ambiguous. On the one hand, it indicates that there is meaning; and on the other, it seems to destroy this conclusion. On the one hand, it seems to point to the concerned God, and on the other, it seems to deny this basic belief. For belief it is. It is not a proof in the scientific sense of the word. It is a belief, an investigation of existence followed by a conclusion that reaches beyond existence.

In his novel *The Stranger,* Camus tries to create a character who lives on the absolute surface of existence. For him there is no question of life being meaningless or having meaning. It just is there and it has little if any relatedness. The main character, Monsieur Meursault, meanders through life apparently without ever asking any real questions. As he stands by the seashore in Algiers pointing a revolver at some Arabs who have caused him and his friends some trouble, he is aware " that one might fire or not fire — and it would come to absolutely the same thing." [28] After the revolver had been fired and after the sentence of death by guillotine had been duly passed, he maintains the same role. When the priest tries to speak with him he reports that, " I went close up to him and made a last attempt to explain that I'd very little time left, and I wasn't going to waste it on God." [29] In the final count, if one could use the word " hope " at all, " all that remained to hope was that on the day of my execution there should be a huge crowd of spectators and that they should greet me with howls of execration." [30] We respond to *The Stranger,* for we too are aware of the negativities of existence that appear to deny that God is concerned.

In *Waiting for Godot,* Samuel Beckett takes an important step beyond *The Stranger.* He too pictures individuals for whom life has no apparent meaning. All that has to be done is to live from moment to moment, day to day, uncertain if there is any relatedness or meaning. But the two tramps, Estragon and Vladimir, are waiting through the meaninglessness, for they have a vague feeling that it might turn out to be something after all. They are waiting for Godot. This is their only purpose as they perform the roles of apparently meaningless existence. After Godot has failed them twice and the play draws to a close without any glimmer of hope the following conversation takes place.

> ESTRAGON: Didi.
> VLADIMIR: Yes.
> ESTRAGON: I can't go on like this.
> VLADIMIR: That's what you think.
> ESTRAGON: If we parted? That might be better for us.
> VLADIMIR: We'll hang ourselves tomorrow. (*Pause*) Unless Godot comes.
> ESTRAGON: And if he comes
> VLADIMIR: We'll be saved.[31]

This puts the situation of existence in a nutshell. Out of the ambiguity of existence we are saved, we are given meaning by belief — by belief in a concerned God. In the end this belief is no more peculiar or strange than not believing. Our existence itself is ambiguous. In either case — belief or disbelief — a person has to take a step beyond existence. On the one hand, he asserts that those elements which point to meaning are real and declares that what he does not understand will eventually be seen as part of the pattern; and on the other, he declares that those which point to meaninglessness are real and all that seems to indicate meaning or purpose will eventually be seen as meaningless too. As has been indicated before, this latter position is rather less tenable because it itself is finally meaningless.

All that can be achieved from a study of our own personal existence is an ambiguous position from which we have to choose one side or the other. But he who decides to take the step of faith soon finds a wealth of material and experience with which to strengthen his belief in the writings of the Scripture and the history of faith. For the writings of Scripture and the history of the church are nothing more than the record of events and individuals' reaction to these events which are expressed in terms of belief rather than meaninglessness. But as one examines and sympathetically studies these records of existence, one is strengthened in one's position and gripped by an awareness of reality that is only dimly apparent when the first step to belief is taken. For these records carry the assertion of men through the ages that God is concerned.

Instinct within the genius of the Christian faith is the concept of God's concern. He is not some far-off, unrelated deity, or one who in a purely irresponsible and capricious way demonstrates his interest in his creation. For the Christian, God's concern is the context in which everything exists. That God is concerned is part of the very givenness of life.

Historically first in the record of the Judaeo-Christian tradition comes the promise to Abraham, "I will make of you a great nation, and I will bless you, and make your name great, so that you will be a blessing" (Gen. 12:2). This is presented again as a promise to Abraham's son Isaac, "Sojourn in this land, and I will be with you, and will bless you" (Gen. 26:3); and it expands from the individual to the social group in Jacob. In the struggle to gain understanding and meaning in life, Jacob comes through his encounter with the deceiver twisted and warped, to become Israel, Prince of God, and through him the people of Israel is blessed. "By you and your descendants shall all the families of the earth bless themselves. Behold, I am with you and will keep you wherever you go." (Gen. 28: 14-15.)

Moses, the stutterer and murderer, has courage to go

and stand before the great Pharaoh to demand freedom for his people because of the promise from God that " I will be with you." From this point on, God is recognized as being involved in the history of Israel. At this initial point of their national history — and it is one to which they continually return with nostalgic longing — they are led through the Red Sea to freedom. The significant point of this Biblical record of history is that the praise is given not to Moses but to God.

> Thus the Lord saved Israel that day from the hand of the Egyptians; and Israel saw the Egyptians dead upon the seashore. And Israel saw the great work which the Lord did against the Egyptians, and the people feared the Lord; and they believed in the Lord and in his servant Moses. (Ex. 14:30-31.)

The " I will bless you " of Abraham and the " I will be with you " of Isaac and Jacob are now closely interwoven with the whole pattern of Hebrew national development. So central does this concept become that it is retold in, and becomes an essential part of, the primitive stories that sought to explain the beginnings of mankind. God walks in the garden and speaks to Adam. He gives his blessing to the man and woman and sees that his creation is good. Even when Adam and Eve, the man and the source of life, rebel against his command and are expelled from the context of their Eden paradise and forced to work their way in the world, God, in a very delightful passage, shows his concern by making them clothes. It is very significant for the whole of Judaeo-Christian thought that even in the situation of punishment, when they had defined themselves out of the context of their true destiny, God is seen as being with them, understanding and concerned.

From the very earliest times this relationship is set in

terms of covenant. A covenant is established with Abraham (Gen. 17:3 ff.), with Isaac, Jacob, Moses, and the Children of Israel. This covenant seeks to spell out in concrete terms what it means to the Hebrew people that they are to live in the context of God's concern. The whole of the history that follows in the Old Testament through the conquering of the Promised Land, the establishment of the kingdom under David, the gradual decline leading eventually to defeat and exile, the return, the destruction and Dispersion, is related to this covenant that is the direct outcome and explication of God's concern. As one studies the history, one realizes that on the one hand men strive to express this covenant in increasingly explicit symbols and on the other they are constantly challenged to relate this concept of the covenant-God's concern to the actual events of this history.

Three agencies served as interpretive functionaries in the social structure of the nation. They were the king, the priests, and the prophets. The king represented the unity of the people of God; the priests established the religious categories of worship and sacrifice in which the context of concern was seen to be expressed; and the prophets, beginning with the ecstatic "sons of the prophets," and always retaining something of that ecstasy, by maintaining the existential relationship to the context, served as critics of king and priests, as interpreters of the changing historical scene, and as the source of creative re-evaluation.

But man was still Adam and, mistaking dominating knowledge for divine wisdom, he began to consider himself as God and to grasp at the context in order to bring it under his control. Kings misunderstood concern as privilege; priests assumed that they had built a definitive structure to give expression to man's relation to the divine concern and that therefore they possessed and had made their own the divine wisdom; and the prophets, forgetful of the existential nature of prophecy, bound themselves to previously established ecstatic patterns and lost their relationship to the real.

Out of the complexities of the prophetic tradition certain men broke through with special insights that revealed something of the depth of the divine concern. The first was Amos proclaiming that righteousness was an essential quality of this context. With violent invective he denounced the social evils of his day and proclaimed the judgment of doom on his nation which had by its living defined itself out of context:

> they sell the righteous for silver,
> and the needy for a pair of shoes –
> (Amos 2:6.)

> I hate, I despise your feasts,
> and I take no delight in your solemn assemblies.
> (Ch. 5:21.)

> Thus says the Lord: "As the shepherd rescues from the mouth of the lion two legs, or a piece of an ear, so shall the people of Israel who dwell in Samaria be rescued, with the corner of a couch and part of a bed." (Ch. 3:12.)

> But let justice roll down like waters,
> and righteousness like an ever-flowing stream.
> (Ch. 5:24.)

Next came Hosea struggling wih his own problem of an unfaithful wife whom he had received back. In truly existential terms he saw his own experience as of the nature of the real and described divine concern not only in terms of justice and punishment but also in terms of continually forgiving love.

Come, let us return to the Lord;
for he has torn, that he may heal us;
he has stricken, and he will bind us up.
(Hos. 6:1.)

When Israel was a child, I loved him,
and out of Egypt I called my son.
The more I called them,
the more they went from me;
they kept sacrificing to the Baals,
and burning incense to idols.
(Ch. 11:1-2.)

How can I give you up, O Ephraim!
How can I hand you over, O Israel!
How can I make you like Admah!
How can I treat you like Zeboiim!
My heart recoils within me,
my compassion grows warm and tender.
I will not execute my fierce anger,
I will not again destroy Ephraim;
for I am God and not man,
the Holy One in your midst,
and I will not come to destroy.
(Vs. 8-9.)

The double blow that eventually destroyed the nation and took its leading citizens into exile was seen by the sensitive prophets as still being delivered within the context of divine concern. It was divine judgment, the counterpart of God's mercy, that raised up the enemy and strengthened his arm. Kingly and priestly structures fell, but the occasional prophetic voice still sounded forth. In the agony of defeat and exile, in the developing hope of salvation and return, and in the re-establishment of the nation the prophetic imagination wove together new strands of understanding concerning the nature of God's relation to his people.

In the declining years of the nation Jeremiah looked forward to the time when a new covenant would be established. This would be given in inwardness freed from the distorting categories of existence.

> But this is the covenant I will make with the house of Israel after those days, says the Lord: I will put my law within them, and I will write it upon their hearts; and I will be their God, and they shall be my people. And no longer shall each man teach his neighbor and each his brother, saying, "Know the Lord," for they shall all know me, from the least of them to the greatest, says the Lord; for I will forgive their iniquity, and I will remember their sin no more. (Jer. 31:33-34.)

But, although there was a definite awareness of God's mercy in the message of the prophets, the exile took place in the atmosphere of tragic despair. " How shall we sing the Lord's song in a foreign land? " moaned the poet as he voiced the loneliness of the lost who had seen punishment as complete removal from the context of his real life.

But mind and spirit stretched in tension came to a new understanding. The " I will be with you " could now be interpreted as applying not only to the holy city of Jerusalem, now destroyed, but also to the exiles in Babylon. Ezekiel presented the new insight in forms of ecstatic vision, while the Second Isaiah presented it in terms of comfort, forgiveness, and salvation.

> But you, Israel, my servant,
> Jacob, whom I have chosen,
> the offspring of Abraham, my friend;
> you whom I took from the ends of the earth,
> and called from its farthest corners,
> saying to you, " You are my servant,
> I have chosen you and not cast you off ";
> fear not, for I am with you,
> be not dismayed, for I am your God;

I will strengthen you, I will help you,
  I will uphold you with my victorious right hand.
    (Isa. 41:8-10.)

From the heights of Isaiah's prophetic insight the reconstituted nation soon was involved in decline. The concern of God was once more set geographically in Jerusalem. Although Habakkuk carried a note of universalism representative of Jeremiah's new covenant, movements of extreme nationalism began to assert themselves. The priestly caste once more established itself as the controller of the divine concern, both politically and spiritually, and the voice of prophecy was all but stifled. Only a few sensitive spirits tried to continue the noble task of relating man to the context of concern. The writer of Jonah presented a dramatic gem that sought to bring back the concept of God's universal concern; and the creator of Job tried to reinterpret the individual's position in the situation of suffering. Neither of them was successful. The control was in the hands of the manipulators of increasingly restrictive rules. The waves of international destruction swept across the small pious nation. But all this disaster was still within the context of concern, and finally the context revealed itself in the coming of the Christ.

Many strands of Jewish thought are woven together in the expectation of the coming of Messiah, or the Christ. Central to the whole expectation was the realization, inherent in their faith and forced home to them in the disastrous nature of their national history, that if life was to have meaning and fulfillment it must come from the inbreaking of God's power. The Book of Daniel, written in a period of great national distress when none of the other symbols, such as king or priest, seemed to have any power, sees the justification and salvation as coming from beyond the human predicament. The " Son of Man " would come riding on the clouds of heaven to justify the faithfulness of his suffering people and to save and re-establish them.

Jesus as the Christ drew together into meaningful pattern all the complex strands of Jewish longing related to life's purpose and meaning in the context of God's concern. He came to the nation of Israel but not in the popularly expected pattern of national sovereignty; in priestly guise he ministered the mysteries of God but not within the expected structures of the priestly code. He himself came as king but with humility; he himself was the Temple in which dwelt the presence of the divine; he himself was the inbreaking of divine power and the Son of Man riding on the clouds of heaven. As prophet he was sensitively aware both of the ambiguities of existence and of the divine word appearing within these ambiguities. Most unexpectedly also he came in the role of the Suffering Servant (Isa., ch. 53), who took upon himself the anxiety, the suffering, and the extinction of death.

All this occurs within the context of divine concern. In this respect the most significant name for Jesus as the Christ is Emmanuel, " God with us." The " I will be with you " that had been recognized as central for life in the early days of Hebrew history and that had always remained as the background of reality, although often misunderstood and misinterpreted, now came into concrete form in the being of the person of Jesus as the Christ.

The awareness of the " presence of the Lord " haunts the Old Testament. It is this awareness which gives meaning to both the individual and the social group of which he is a part. The " presence " is haunting because he is always hidden within the structures of existence. The " presence of the Lord " was in the pillar of fire and of cloud that led the Hebrew slaves to freedom; he was with the kings and priests and prophets; he dwelt in the Ark of the Covenant and in the Holy of Holies in the Temple. His was a haunting "presence," for the pillar vanished, the holy men and leaders often seemed to be directed by nothing more than their own self-interest, the Temple fell, and the Holy of Holies was desecrated. But the "presence" was not destroyed with the destruction of his supposed abode. The "presence" was the Christ, the Logos, the Wisdom, the outgoing expression of God into the dimension of time. And in Jesus the "presence" became actualized as personality. The actions, the words, the understanding, the healing, the agony, and death were all part of the creative activity of God, which was both revelatory and participatory. In both respects it is man's salvation.

No good purpose can be served by a detailed investigation, as has been done many times in Christian thought, of the relation of the human and divine natures in Jesus as the Christ. Where this has been done it has led to a sharp distinction between certain psychological qualities that are declared to be divine and others that are seen as human. The result has been that man himself has been dichotomized, with the elements of his so-called "human nature" appearing worthless and even negative, and the "divine" attributes as being of infinite worth. But man cannot be split. He remains man even although he may seek to deny a part of his humanity. The separation of the divine and human in Jesus as the Christ has always led to a denial of his complete participation either in the divine or the human. An adoptionist Christology which emphasizes that Jesus earned the position of the Christ by his perfect humanity throws man back to a reliance upon his own human striving for his fulfillment; and a completely docetic Christology which holds that humanity had no part to play in this process of salvation strips man himself, as he is in his human predicament, of any meaning.

There is no purpose in applying the psychoanalytic method to Jesus as the Christ. What happens in his coming is an event beyond the categories of this method and incommensurable with its concepts and techniques. Paul Tillich, who points to the dimension of depth that is revealed to man in the coming of the Christ, is stressing the unity of the human and the divine in the " New Being."

> The term " New Being," as used here, points directly to the cleavage between essential and existential being — and is the restorative principle of the whole of the theological system. The New Being is new in so far as it is the undistorted manifestation of essential being within and under the conditions of existence. It is new in two respects: it is new in contrast to the merely potential character of essential being; and it is new over and against the estranged character of existential being. It is actual, conquering the estrangement of actual existence.[32]

In Christ is established " God-man hood " which is the relationship that is man's true destiny.

It is important to underscore the fact that this is no man-made fulfillment. The New Being that conquers the estrangement of existence is not a psychological state that man can reach by his own efforts. The coming of Jesus as the Christ, the establishment within time of the New Being, is the expression of God's concern for man in existence.

> In the beginning was the Word, and the Word was with God, and the Word was God. He was in the beginning with God; all things were made through him, and without him was not anything made that was made. In him was life, and the life was the light of men. (John 1:1-4.)

This is a very significant passage. Here is the cosmic God creating through his Word. Although this is set in the context of Greek logos philosophy in which the logos was the principle in all creation, yet a new concept is added. Logos means " word." Word is the extension of the personality, the outgoing quality that creates as it is uttered. The word of command or the word of compassion is the direct outgoing of the personality giving expression to its very being. So the outgoing word of God is seen as the extension of his being. By this power were all things created. By this word are all things held together. Then comes the essential and significant part of the Christian message. *The Word became flesh.* In Christ the power that creates the cosmos and that sustains all things actually became man.

To our scientific objective minds here is a strange and amazing message. The God of all space actually occupied our space. The limited, finite, uninformed, feeble, and bigoted space we occupy has been occupied by the creative Word of God. He is aware of our frustrations, our anxieties, our pains, our agony, our vision, our planning, our mediocrity, our courage; for he has submitted himself to the limitations of our time-bound life and has suffered the experience of nonbeing that we call death. He has suffered and risen victorious. The victory of being — creativity, compassion, concern, eternity, infinitude, right, truth, justice, and life is asserted over negativity, hatred, time, finitude, evil, and death. It is asserted in the final and authoritative way when Christ was raised from the dead.

This, after all, is the main message of the gospel. Life, true life, has conquered death; meaning has overcome meaninglessness; concern has overcome the objective mechanization; justice has overcome wrong; and good stands supreme over evil.

It is amazing that so much of our modern religion is concerned with morality. Petty moral problems are the constant source of pulpit material until people are completely wearied with petty moralism. They have become so used to it that they expect it and do not even bother to go to church because they know already what will be said. Morality is a part of the total message, but it is an incidental part, and a part that should logically be automatic. The Gospels spend very little time on moralizing, and where it is mentioned the main sections are directed against the religious people of the day who had the proud belief that they were the moral and godly people. The shock, when they found that they were not, was so great they crucified their critic. In so doing, they set the stage for the revelation of God that we call Christian.

One third of the Gospels is concerned with the last week of Jesus' life. The events surrounding the crucifixion and the resurrection are given pride of place. Here was an event on the stage of history that completely gripped the minds of men. In it they saw, dramatically portrayed, the answer to their deepest need. Here was the proof that God, the creator of all things, was concerned. We can never divest this of the element of drama. It is apparent that a coldly logical investigation can produce nothing of significance. All that this approach can say is that a young upstart, impatient with the religious machinery of the day, expressed himself too vociferously and brought upon himself the condemnation of those whom he attacked. By the subtle association of circumstances in which the occupying power, represented by Pontius Pilate, was anxious to maintain good relations with the religious leaders of the conquered nation, represented by the high priest, the young man was subsequently put to death by the accepted method decreed for non-Roman Jews, which was crucifixion. Some of his followers declared that he was alive, but this was discounted because the vast majority of people, including his judge and his accusers, never saw him again.

And yet, let us face it frankly, in and through these events a new era had begun. There were people now convinced that God had revealed his true nature, that the final questions of the world and of life had now received their answer. There were people who were convinced that in and through these events the fact had been demonstrated that being had conquered nonbeing, that life had overcome death, that meaning had overcome meaninglessness. And these people, unintelligent, uninformed, not represented in the powerful courts of the day, yet began a new era in human history.

The cross stands at the very center of the Christian faith. In that event something became nothing and from the combination rose a new being. In the event, which is manifestly absurd, although the reasons for its occurrence can *post factum* be easily defined, both the rational and the absurd were united to form a new thing that actually can nevermore be a thing but a person with whom we are related.

For him who lives this faith, then, the categories of the rational and the absurd, the something and the nothing, are all included. Even the judgments of meaning and meaninglessness are held in abeyance. Beyond all these categories, actually including them, are life and God. Thus man's response in every situation of life is to live and worship. His participation in the present is to live and worship. Living he acts here and now, and worshiping he relates himself to him who eventually determines his destiny.

The death of Christ is then seen not as the natural rational outcome of a judicial procedure against a rebel but as the acceptance of man's categories of rational and nonrational in the being of God himself; involvement in our human judgments of meaning and meaninglessness. Here the final drama for all time is enacted because God is concerned. And the resurrection stands then as the assertion of a new reality, the actuality of a new being involved both in the rational and the absurd, the something and the nothing.

7

Living in Context

The context provides meaning. A word alone is meaningless. It is a sound without an environment, an assembly of letters without relevance. An act alone is meaningless. It is a series of movements without purpose. A man standing on a line waving a flag is ridiculous unless we know that he is an official in the football game. " Life " is a word, but it is merely an assembly of letters without relevance unless the context is known. " Life " is a series of movements, but the movements are ridiculous unless the environment in which they have meaning is recognized.

Modern man is uncertain about his context. He is proudly convinced that he can define it himself, but he continually becomes involved in an inescapable logical frustration. He himself is part of the context that he seeks to describe to himself. Indeed, the fact that he generally sees himself as the center of this context makes his task of understanding it pathetically futile. To describe it he has to remove himself and stand outside his own context. This is an obvious recipe for schizophrenia.

There are many agencies trying to define the context for modern man. The sociologists describe the structure of his society, physicists are concerned with the structure of his physical world, physiologists and psychologists endeavor to describe the structure of his body and his mind. A considerable amount of man's time and intelligence is dedicated to a determined effort to find out the facts of his context. Higher and higher grow the stacks of accumulated data about the context until they must be microfilmed for storage. So convinced has man become that the accumulation of facts will develop his knowledge and thus lead to an understanding of his context that he has completely forgotten the purpose of his study and bows in worship before the god of fact. The high priests of the new religion are the mechanics of the computing machines and electronic brains that digest and evaluate masses of material that man with his puny mind could never hope to understand.

But a fear grips the heart of man when he finds that he too comes through the transistor relays of his electronic brain in the form of a number and a punched card. He suddenly becomes aware that he is just that — an accumulation of data on a punched card — or else his worship of the almighty statistic is extremely superficial and is in no way leading him to an understanding of his true context.

The sociologist who may present an expert and stimulating analysis of man's society often finds it extremely difficult to draw his data to a conclusion. *The Organization Man* is a revealing survey of the situation in which mid-twentieth-century man finds himself. It is significant that the closing appendix is dedicated to the edifying topic of "How to Cheat on Personality Tests." Those who probe deeper come through with anxious paradoxes. Riesman writes of "The Lonely Crowd"; Fromm of "Escape from Freedom"; Carrel, in the age of facts, of "Man, the Unknown," and Johnson analyzes modern sophisticated mankind as " People in Quandaries."

Still deeper probing leads us to the philosophers and the dramatists and the novelists who cannot escape the cry of despair. Toynbee still has some hope, but it is a resigned, scarcely believing hope, presented in a dream as a man clings to the cross in a majestic cathedral, and the words written in Latin are "wait and pray." Jaspers sees gloom as he writes: " A dread of life perhaps unparalleled in its intensity is modern man's sinister companion." [33] The epitaph for Willie Loman in *Death of a Salesman* is spoken by his misunderstood and misunderstanding son, " You know something, Charley, there's more of him in that front stoop than all the sales he ever made." [34] Camus calls for the Spartan existence. More and more Greek plots are resurrected to describe heroic modern man fighting out his tragedy with fate. " The Myth of Sysiphus " is the story of a man eternally engaged in perspiring frustration as he rolls his rock to the height of the mountain only to have it crash to the valley whenever he nears the summit.

Kafka sets his hero K on a fruitless search. He is appointed to a position that does not exist, in a village in which he is neither welcome nor understood, employed by masters in the castle whom he does not know and who will not see him. *The Castle* records his fruitless endeavors to be accepted in the village on the one hand and to reach his employers in the castle on the other. The book is the completely irrelevant record of his continued and absolute failure to find any context in which his life, his work, or his existence has meaning.

The cry of despair that dominates the modern scene of letters is a forthright declaration that the context of life that man has defined for himself is inadequate. He gazes at the machine that he has made, aware that he is being dominated by its efficiency, and senses that he has somehow lost his birthright in its powerful production. He regards the structures of power that he has formed, which continually threaten and even demand the sacrifice of his life, and cries the cry of loneliness of the mass man. Man-meaning has been swallowed up in questionable mass-meaning. The rootlessness, the lostness, the fearful sense of meaninglessness of modern man is the unconscious assertion that the context that he has chosen for himself is not his true context. As the river carrying too much water for its carefully set banks overflows and obliterates its channel and spreads havoc, so man refusing to be bound to his cultural context wanders lost and destructive.

The word " God " stands for the context of life. In this sense everyone has his god who is the context of his life and in relation to whom his life has meaning. Faith is the relation of trust established between man and the context of his life, and worship is the continual process of self-commitment by which a man completely involves himself and his life in this context. In this sense religion is a natural quality of man. It is not something peculiar and strange. All his life man is religious. Religion means " binding back " to the context of meaning. It is the word that points to man's relation to his god, the context of his life.

It is apparent that man has considerable freedom in choosing the context in which he will consciously live his life. Although much of his life is given to him from his ultimate and real context he can determine for himself the nature of his functional context, and in so doing defines both his god and the meaning and purpose of his life.

A man may define success as the functional context in which his life has meaning. Success then becomes his god.

Daily he worships at this shrine. He immerses himself in this context and binds himself to it by the power of faith. In turn he himself is defined by this context. Since he has defined his context as success, the only relevant statement that can be made about his life is in these terms. He may also define his god as public acclaim. This is the context in which he sees life as meaningful. His whole life is directed toward constructing situations in which he will receive acclaim and honor. His unuttered prayer is that he may gain this recognition; and this prayer is constant. He dedicates himself and his life at this altar, training and developing his talents, giving mind, energy, time, and money as sacrifice toward establishing himself firmly in the context in which he sees his life as real.

Family, money, nation, pleasure, sport, knowledge — there is no end to the number of functional contexts that man can single out for himself and make his god. The temptation to idolatry is continually present.

The claim of the Christian church is that the real context of true life is God as shown to us in Jesus who is the Christ. " The Christ " is a title, the Greek equivalent of the Hebrew " Messiah." And for the Hebrews, completely baffled by life, unhappy, unsuccessful, unrecognized, the messiah was to be the revealer of the true God, the source of the full relation to man's real context.

The idolatrous gods whom we so easily worship are fickle tyrants who eventually reject the man who has given his life to their worship. Sooner or later the successful man is proved unsuccessful. It may be in the course of his life that his limited deity denies him his place in that context, or it may be only at his most successful funeral that the failure of his life is revealed. The man who worships at the shrine of public acclaim is eventually defeated or retired and only comes to light from time to time as a peculiar antique. He who binds himself solely to family eventually finds himself alone. The organization, to which man may dedicate all his life, has no memory; the machine in whose employ he has found his meaning has no sympathy for his dying strength except to dispense tranquilizer pills when the appropriate button is pressed.

The Christian church does not define God in a way that he can be grasped by man and used in the development of his human purposes. The Christian church stands as a constant witness that God is God, that the true context of our life is always beyond our manipulation and control. The church provides an environment in which man can worship, can confess his idolatry, and relate himself to the true context in which his life is real.

The Christian faith places man in a context that is cosmic. In space no limitations are placed upon the environment in which his life is meaningful. While there are many structures in the cosmos that he may use to give himself a place, he distorts his true nature if he makes these definitive. The environment of the family, of the career, of the organization, of the city, of the nation, are all elements of the cosmos in which man finds a place. But he denies his soul's heritage if he defines himself only within these structures. His vision becomes distorted, his judgment biased, his longing for life eventually unfulfilled unless he relates himself and his being to the whole of the ordered structure of being.

This context is creative. In relation to this context, the Christian faith claims that man fulfills his creative purpose. In any context man can exercise a creative power. In so far as his work is related to the creative power of his true context it is real. In so far as it is not related to this true context it is unreal.

This context is concerned. It is neither mechanical nor remote, being involved in the process of life. In the temporary success and the frequent disasters that arise in his idolatry, man's true context is involved. Man can never fully withdraw himself from the context of his life, just as he can never withdraw himself from the air he breathes. And the concerned context participates in his suffering and the cramped agony that follows his imprisonment by idolatry.

For the Christian faith God is this context. He is the ground of all being. By his creative word everything that exists is brought into existence and endowed with the possibility of truly creative change. He is concerned that everything that exists fulfills its purpose and relates itself to its true context. To this end he has revealed his nature and to man this revelation comes in the person of Jesus as the Christ. It is in relation to him that man finds his place in his true context and his life becomes instinct with the creativity that is real.

God is the real. For our world of four-dimensional time and space he by his being defines the real. The nature of his involvement in our existence defines for us the nature of participation in reality. Human activity, or creativity, of itself is not automatically real. No matter how vigorous it may be, no matter how successful it may appear to be it is not, on this account, necessarily real. Even the most sincere and most energetic activity of man can actually carry the mask of unreality. Only that is real which is related to the self-involvement of God who in his creativity defines the real.

The Christian faith holds that God is involved in existence, that he is actually the context in which we stand forth meaningfully. By the creative power of God we come into existence and in relation to this creativity man defines his own meaningfulness or meaninglessness. This faith holds that God's outgoing creative power, analogically his Word, is continually expressing his will within existence. All men who are related closely to this creative Word direct us to reality. But the definitive expression of this creativity of God was made in the person of Jesus as the Word of God in human flesh.

Christians frequently claim that Jesus is the great example. This claim is both true and false. It is true in that Jesus as the Christ is the definitive expression of reality within existence set in the time and place in which he lived. It is false in so far as the believer holds that the actual events and actions of Jesus in the first century A.D. define events and actions that are always real and that by patterning one's life religiously according to events and teachings of Jesus' life man is enabled to inject himself into the stream of reality.

A man lives in his time and the events of his life are unique, not only in their occurrence but in the fact that they occur for him in his time. It is within this situation that he must live. Within this situation he has the possibility of being real. He creates unreality if he tries to cast his experiences in first-century terms, with the basic assumption that the events of every life somehow repeat the events of the years A.D. 30 to 33, and then provide himself with a quick answer to living by acting as Jesus acted in the comparable circumstance.

The life and teachings of Jesus are the examples, in that these events and sayings dramatically portray the actions of one who in these particular situations and events acted and spoke reality. True drama involves the audience as participant. He who is involved in the events and teachings of Jesus' life — and for us now we can only be involved dramatically — has the experiential involvement by which he can live in his own situation in a real way. In this sense, and this alone, Jesus is our example.

Primarily he is, in and through the events of his life and especially the events of Easter week, our Savior. This is in a completely different category from that of the exemplar theology. As we have said, man is continually tempted to define his own context, to create his own god, and in relation to this created deity to define reality in idolatrous and unreal terms. In the gospel story of Jesus as the Christ we see the creatively real submitting himself to the patterns of idolatry, suffering extinction under their cancerous growth, and rising victor over the power of the unreal.

The worship of the Christian church and especially the Communion service involves the believer in this pattern of events. In the Sacrament he is actually incorporated in the process of extinction to the power of unreality, and of life by the power of the real.

When Paul speaks of being " in Christ " he is speaking of involvement in the creative activity of the real that bears the condemnation of idolatrous unreality even to submitting to extinction in existence. In Christ a man becomes created anew. Again, as in the very process of his standing forth into existence when he derives his reality from the creative power of his context, so he is re-created by this same power in the context of the real.

The Christian faith is always instant to point out that this is not a result of man's striving, although he constantly strives to find the real even in his idolatrous wonderings, nor is it a reward of his taking Jesus as his example, although he will seek to be dramatically involved in Jesus' life and teachings. This re-creation comes about from the creative activity of the Word of God himself who involves man. He who is " in Christ " is then saved from the power of his own unreal idolatry and is transferred to the reality of the creative context of God who defines the real.

This, of course, provides an example of a different dimension although not necessarily of a different quality. As the Christian is involved in the suffering and extinction of the Christ, so he is able to be involved in the suffering and complete or partial extinction of his desires and himself under the power of unreality with the confidence that the real is victorious. In fact, he is quite aware that there are powers of idolatrous unreality in himself and in his world that he must bear or suffer in the process of being related to the real. The Christian is aware of both Creation and Fall. He knows that within existence unreality threatens the real and that he is involved in the unreality even though he be related to the real and that conflict and suffering are involved in the victory. Thus he will be expectant though not fearful of suffering, for he is involved both in cross and resurrection.

In this way Christ is Savior. It is his power, demonstrated in the events of the gospel story, that in each instant is capable of relating man to the real. In this he saves him from his idolatrous involvement.

In *Endgame,* Beckett pictures the end in the context of despair. The main character, blind and confined to a wheel chair, dominates the stage. His servant, completely dominated by the irrelevant demands of his master, always longs to leave, but there is no place to go. The old parents never move out of their assigned place in the garbage cans at the side of the stage.

It is the basis of the Christian faith that this life despite all its apparent meaninglessness and its absurdity is meaningful. But it has meaning only in the context of God. In so far as the world is related to him, the ground of being, it is meaningful. In so far as it is not related, it is meaningless. In so far as we are in the true context of God we live, and in so far as we are not in this context, die. Sin, separation, estrangement, meaninglessness, are all words that describe categories of existence out of context.

The desire of every man is to be in context, and it is the sole purpose of the church to be the instrument by which mankind is set in his true context. Admittedly the church does not always recognize this. Religion can be presented as an opiate to dull the sensibilities of the uneasy conscience or the anxious heart. It can concern itself with making people feel happy, of raising up questions that were disturbing fifty years ago and providing archaic answers so that those who have not bothered to keep their religious sensitivities alive feel that they have the solution to their problems.

There is no place here for setting down rules and regulations. Sometimes the church likes to feel secure by establishing clearly its patterns of acceptance. The modern evangelist sets it all in the framework of repentance and conversion. And there is a place for this in the church. But the people we venerate in the gospel stories by no means all went through this pattern. The shepherds and the kings whom we represent each Christmas, related to the Christ by the expectation in their hearts, came with adoration, joy, and gifts. There are no words of repentance but only joy as they related themselves to the object of their search. The disciples came with their questions and their doubts and the longings in their souls and related themselves to their master whom they came to adore. The centurion came out of the detailed duty of his office asking help for his son, and Jesus spoke to his disciples of the centurion's great faith.

It is clear that Jesus associated with the sinners who were gripped by the power of the new context in which they found themselves. All the way through the significant step was a relation in context, which is the act of faith. Then a man born blind steps out of the gloom and is given sight by his relation to this new context. And while all the religious men struggle to place the guilt — did this man sin or his parents — Jesus points out that this question is irrelevant. " It was not that this man sinned, or his parents, but that the works of God might be made manifest in him." (John 9:3.)

When the man whose son was mad came seeking help the question was not, " Have you confessed your sin? "; plainly and simply it was, " Do you believe? " And the man was honest. He was aware of the conflicts that tore his mind and he replied, " I believe; help my unbelief! " (Mark 9:24). Surely this is one of the most universal statements in the whole Bible.

There is no set pattern. The church does wrong if it seeks to set rigid rules for the Christian experience. The only things that stand out, if we wish to make a generalization, are a sense of need and a relation of faith.

" Confess your sins " is a typical religious phrase, and the church is always tempted to set about spelling out the sins down to the smallest minutiae, so that each man can be aware of his sin. But the procedure becomes so complex that all the time can be taken up working on the category of sins. But for the people of the gospel "confess your sins" is "realize your need," "Be aware that you are out of touch with your true context and that hand in hand with it and intimately woven into the same realization is a relation in context by the act of faith."

Cogito ergo sum, wrote Descartes, and set the stage for the whole of modern rationalism that reaches its latest bitter fruit in logical positivism. *Respondeo ergo sum,* writes Heinemann, summing up and advancing the position of the response school and writing a psychological metaphysic, "I reach reality; I am real; I have reality, in so far as I respond, and in so far as my responses become answers." [35] But for the Christian it is *fideo ergo sum.* I believe; I have faith; I am in relation in context of life, therefore, I am real.

The difficulty here is to find a symbol that will avoid the categories of subjectivism on the one hand and of objectivism on the other. The *cogito* steps completely into the world of the subjective and the *respondeo,* no matter how Heinemann may endeavor to place it in the preconscious, always assumes an object. *Fideo* points to a creative state of relation. In its primary form it precedes the categories of subject and object. It is man in relation. Faith is the intimate relation that places man in the ground of being and makes him real. It is mystery, which means the closing of the eyes and the closing of the ears, allowing neither subject nor object.

Barth calls it the "grasped grasp" and Tillich the state of being grasped by ultimate concern. This points to the context as the place of faith. It is not a response to stimuli. It is an awareness of the need of context if we would be real and the state of relatedness in that context which comes as air filling the vacuum of our need.

This faith has no relation to supposed proof that God exists or to the contrary proof that God does not exist. The futility of being involved in this type of purely logical reasoning is well demonstrated by Dostoevsky's character who proves to his own satisfaction that God does not exist. His logic then proceeds as follows: first, if God does not exist, then he is God; second, if he is God and God does not exist, he must cease to exist in order to be God; third, he commits a perfectly logical suicide in order to fill his divine destiny.

Religious people must move their forces out of this battlefield and leave it, if you will, as a Pyrrhic victory to the modern " God does not exist " battalions. They stand victorious in a field that they have already defined as "meaningless," " absurd," and " nothing." And we should take our stand again where the witness of the religious writers would direct us — to the basic reality that God is. He is, and in this context we are real.

Worship

The primary need for man in the modern age is to worship the true God. Man is a worshiping creature. He always worships. In general he worships at the shrine of his own created deities. He bows before the semi-real idol that his puny mind and his self-centered spirit can comprehend. He accepts as his deity a fraction god and strives to complete the integer by his own powers. In the process he deifies himself and bows before the throne on which he and his abilities sit in power.

His primary task in the present day and at all times is to take the step beyond Camus and acknowledge that God is God. This means that he recognizes that he is man, only made in the image of God, and that God is with him and encounters him at every moment of his existence. God is the source and ground of his being and the context in which his life has meaning. In relation to this context he acknowledges his dependence, his utter dependence, and he worships.

Worship is the act by which man acknowledges his humanity, his temporality, his frailty, and his need of help. It is the action by which he states that he is not God and asks God for guidance. Worship begins with adoration. Adoration is the open recognition of God's power and deity, of his reality and his nature as the ground of all being. Worship is the act of recognizing that God has given us life, intelligence, and will with which we function in existence in this world of time and space.

Worship follows with confession. We have done that which is not pleasing in thy holy sight. We have endeavored to make ourselves God. Continually we have assumed that we are the director of the play of life and that, by careful manipulation, we can manage the actors on life's stage. We can rule our own deities. We have power over the destinies of others. By verbal manipulation and a sound motivational analysis we direct the destinies of masses of mankind. By the careful analysis of events along a unidimensional time scale we can establish our sovereignty over the lives and purpose of others. We have cast man and nature into one mechanical process and have proceeded to dominate and control their destinies by our almighty power — whether they be our children, our customers, or our constituency. On the stage of life we have thought to become directors and have forgotten the dimension of perspective that shows us to be only part players.

We repent and we seek the forgiveness of thy grace.

> Almighty God, who doth freely pardon all who repent and turn to him, now fulfill in every contrite heart the promise of redeeming grace; remitting all our sins, and cleansing us from an evil conscience; through the perfect sacrifice of Jesus Christ our Lord.[36]

The place where the Christian becomes most significantly involved in worship is in the sacrament of Communion. This symbol is central and it is a symbol in which the worshiper is involved dramatically. In this service all that has been written here of true life being destroyed by the power of dominating objectification and yet rising victorious is symbolized and re-enacted with the worshiper as participant. The body is broken and the blood is poured out; the objective thing is destroyed. But that which cannot be objectified, the life in its real form, is not destroyed and is victorious over the threat of meaninglessness and nonbeing. The Christian church sees this service as the drama-symbol by which man in existence is related to true life, to the context in which his life has meaning if he is involved in the drama by the act of faith.

AND LIVE

Worship is the activity by which man is related to the context of reality. Living is the activity by which he expresses his mediated creativity in his own environment of history.

Living must be differentiated from existing. " Existing " expresses a state. It is the state of standing out of the ground of being. It describes the state in which man finds himself in relation to reality. To say " I exist " is then merely to make a descriptive statement of the static state. " Existence " is a term devoid of meaning unless recognition is given to the ground from which one " stands out." To develop a so-called " philosophy of existence " that has no place for the ground of standing out is to engage in a mere accumulation of words, which, no matter how grammatically correct may be their grouping, is finally meaningless.

For man existence is the state in which living becomes possible. " Living " is a dynamic term that carries with it the sense of purpose and fulfillment. It also implies a significant relation with the ground out of which one exists.

If it is possible to act in the state of existing without reference to the ground, the result is merely acting. It is a play on a meaningless stage. When this is done one performs the actions of an automaton and life becomes completely functional. There is abundant evidence that this is very much the character of our modern scene. On all sides there is the tendency for the dynamic life to be differentiated down to the state of existence. In this the purpose of life is defined in such functional terms as production and the process is to be spelled out in terms of functional activity. Thus Camus can hold up a mirror to modern man and show him " Jean Baptiste Clamence–play actor." [37]

Although existence is a prerequiste of living for man, it does not control or direct life. It is merely the necessary structure in which the dynamic of life can appear. Living, in the terms of this essay, is the expressing of the real within the structures of existence. It is the appearing of being itself; it is the actualization in time and space of the true context.

Living is then a religious process. It is the result of man's being bound back to the context in which he has meaning.

There is a continual temptation to deny this dependence and to assert that man himself has the power of living.

When this is done man is left with only the structures. In relation to the structures of existence he can be classified as a conformist or a rebel. Although it may demand energy and the experience may be termed "life," yet in this activity man has devalued himself to the level of a serviceman of the structures endeavoring either to maintain or to replace or change superficial elements of the structures of existence. The tragedy of this devaluation is the horror of our time.

In the latter half of the twentieth century, man is becoming a creature of conformity. He is expected to tailor himself to the structures that are already established. In all nations of the world this is the pattern; under the legal force of totalitarianism and under the social pressures of democracy he is expected to conform. Within the home and community he is expected to fit a pattern. All types of advertising condition him to fulfill the prescribed role. Throughout the world he is expected to adhere to the principles of nationalism and to sacrifice his life for the sanctity of this concept.

In our present stage of Western culture, man is trained to fit into the pattern of the organization, just as in a totalitarian country he is trained to take his place in the structure of the state. The temptation is great for the organization man to think he finds meaning in the structures of organization and for totalitarian man to find meaning in the structures of his totalitarian society. In the latter this is actually taught; in the former it is frequently implied. When man succumbs to or is educated into this temptation he does not live. He merely exists in the static state of structure. In the extreme case he defines himself solely in existence, manipulates the structures, immerses himself in form, and defines himself in terms of separation from his real context. This is hell in its true form, and its threatening bell rings for us in every prophetic work of modern art that is solely concerned with form, texture, and the scientific placing of color. There is form without context, structure without relationship, existence without meaning. Nonobjective art in its formalism points to the tendency in our age for man to become committed solely to existence and its structures. Sterile, noncreative, static, and dead can be the judgment upon our age unless life is given opportunity to breathe.

The structures of existence are necessary. They are the environment in which life is lived. It is futile for man to expect to find life merely by escaping. It may be that he will rebel against particular aspects of his existence because he senses that they threaten to stifle life. But new patterns will develop. As long as he is in existence he must expect its structures.

Life can be lived in whatever structures may exist. Life may be lived in the closed walls of a prison as well as on the open plains, in the canyon walls of a great city as well as in the pleasant spaces of suburbia. For life is a result of a relationship with the true context.

For man in existence, living is creating and living is concern. The direction of life is always out, filling up as it were the vacuum in the structures. And as such, life with its creativity and concern is crucified by the harsh objectivity of existence. Life is continually self-giving even to the point of death. Man does not live by what he takes to himself but only by what he gives out. The movement of life is out and the motto of life is give.

Living, then, is a quality beyond existence. It is living in the context of the symbol of death and life. He who truly participates in the drama of the Sacrament in the communion of believers, then, is a person in space time who continually bears the mark of this participation. This means that all the activities of objectification, all the assemblage of facts with which he will be concerned, are in no way of ultimate concern. He will treat the structures of existence seriously. The patterns of social structure, the events that occur upon the plain of history, the tensions of mankind, the thrill of creative experiment, the problems of nations, the needs of the city, the anxious struggle for self-satisfaction of man will be for him serious aspects of existence in which he must be fully involved. But his involvement will be definitely colored by his participation in the drama of the death and life Sacrament.

He knows that he is objectified and that he himself objectifies. He is aware that at every moment he may and does succumb to the temptation to dominate, to make himself god, or to be dominated. He is aware that he must continually see life in the symbol of the Sacrament where dominating objectivity has exerted its power and been conquered and through this he is given forgiveness.

And so he immerses himself in the common life — in the market place, in the courts, in the schools, in the church, in the halls of justice and of government. He is aware that through all these the creative spirit of God is at work, and that, for him, in his involvement there is meaning for his life and forgiveness for his sin.